American Muscle Cars

William G. Holder
and Phillip Kunz

TAB BOOKS

Blue Ridge Summit, PA

NOTE: Due to typographical error on page 2 of the color section, a 1967 Camaro is identified as a 1987 model.

FIRST EDITION
FIRST PRINTING

© 1992 by **TAB Books**.
TAB Books is a division of McGraw-Hill, Inc.

Library of Congress Cataloging-in-Publication Data

Holder, William G., 1937–
    American muscle cars / by William G. Holder and Phillip Kunz.
       p.   cm.
    Includes index.
    ISBN 0-8306-2076-1 (h)
    1. Muscle cars—United States—History.   I. Kunz, Phillip.
  II. Title.
  TL23.H65 1991
  629.222′0973—dc20   91-21717
                                        CIP

TAB Books offers software for sale. For information and a catalog, please contact TAB Software Department, Blue Ridge Summit, PA 17294-0850.

Acquisitions Editor: Kimberly Tabor
Technical Editor: Steve Mesner
Production: Katherine G. Brown
Book Design: Joanne Slike

There's a lot of work and time involved in putting together a collection of data such of this. Thanks to my wife Ruthann for putting up with me during those hundreds of hours.

Contents

Acknowledgments

It's difficult to adequately thank all the people who offered both assistance and advice in the assembling of this book. As the book was put together, new aspects of the muscle car sport became evident and the need for data—and the verification of that data—became necessary. The help I received from a large list of experts across the country is appreciated beyond words. I hope that I didn't forget anybody, but if I did, you know who you are.

For assistance in the General Motors area, thanks go to Jim Wirth (former president of the U.S. Camaro Club), Tom Boyd (Camaro expert), Rob Farmer (Buick), Mac DeMere and Paul Zazarine (Corvette), Tom Kitchen (Chevy 409), Tom Migut and Wayne Bushey (National Nostalgic Nova Club), George Lyons (Chevelle), Dennis Casteel (Oldsmobile), Ed and Elizabeth Saudys (Oldsmobile Club of America), Bill Hale (Pontiac Trans-Am), and Fran Preve (Chevy engines).

In the Ford arena, great thanks must go to the always-helpful France and Charles Crites of the Performance Ford Club of America, Marvin Scothorn (Mustang), Vic Brown (Mustang), Mike Besecker (Mercury), and Dr. John Craft, whom I respect as one of the true Ford experts in the country.

With Chrysler muscle cars, I always look to Larry Bell, whose knowledge of these cars seems to flow on forever. He was a real motivator to me in this effort. Then there is Tony DePillo, a builder of these cars and an expert of the highest order. Finally, a word of thanks to George Cone, the expert on Chrysler 300s.

Jeff Kennedy helped greatly on the American Motors models. David Tucker and John Farquhar are to be thanked for photography.

Thanks, everybody!

Preface

It's been the biggest explosion ever in the car collecting hobby! Who would ever have guessed that the high-performance cars of the 1960s and early 1970s — cars that could hardly be given away during the gas crunch days of the 1970s — would have evolved into *the* collectibles of the 1980s and 1990s?

Who knows why this phenomenon took place? Who would have guessed that these machines — formerly called "impractical" and "fuel-guzzling" — would suddenly turn to pure gold? Maybe it was due to the aging of the generation that was in its teens and twenties when these cars were new. Now, 20 years later, the financial means are available to these people to acquire — or reacquire — the performance dream cars of their youth. In many cases, a car was bought initially for nostalgic reasons, and then it suddenly became valuable.

Granted, the performance cars of today are just as fast as their vintage counterparts, but it was the *way* the vintage machines made their horsepower: with monstrous cubic inches and carburetors, thank you — no turbos, no fuel injection systems or superchargers.

There are those who look at the muscle car hobby strictly from a profit-making point of view, even to the point of faking desirable cars with engine swaps and the appropriate trim changes. But to the true enthusiast, the classic magnetism of these cars far exceeds even their financial benefits. They are unforgettable with their sight and sound of power. The throaty rumble of those monstrous mills translated into neck-snapping performance that did and does excite the soul.

Introduction

What exactly *is* a muscle car? It's a term that has several definitions. Let's examine some of them.

To most muscle car enthusiasts, massive cubic inches are the number-one requirement. During the 1960s and early 1970s—a time we'll call the "performance era"—big-block powerplants of over 400 cubic inches were the "in" thing when mated with sleek, "race car" styling.

But other types of cars also fall into the muscle car category, in some minds. How about a big family four-door car with that same big powerplant? Isn't that a muscle car?

Another category of cars that fall into the ill-defined boundaries of the muscle car hobby are the so-called "pony cars." These often featured smaller engines than the aforementioned cars—usually 350 cubic inches or less—but fitted with elaborate carburetion systems or high-performance internal parts to pump up the horsepower.

The real muscle car in most minds, however, is the car with a big-cubic-inch powerplant resting under the hood of a small or midsize body. Maybe the most objective standards would be the power-to-weight ratio of the model or the actual performance capability of the car.

In this book, we'll consider *all* those definitions, because all the different categories are muscle machines of a sort. None should be omitted, since automobiles of this type will never be built again. High-performance cars will be built, but that power will never be produced in the same way it was in the "performance era" muscle cars.

It was an exciting time in American automotive history, the likes of which will probably never be seen again. It was a time when performance was measured in good old cubic inches, which were often proudly displayed on the front fenders. More was better, and "too much" was just about right. There were few fuel injection systems and no turbos during this time period. The brute power of these machines was produced solely by deep-drinking carburetors.

Several other influences during the 1960s and early 1970s prompted the muscle car craze. The Big Three car companies were actively involved in both drag and oval-track racing, and both influenced the design of the street cars of the time. Then, too, gas cost about 30 cents a gallon, which didn't discourage the development of gas-gulping big-block engines.

This book will attempt to provide a basic understanding of the muscle car craze. When possible, production figures for each model will be provided. It should be noted, however, that there is much argument about the accuracy of some of the figures. We'll provide the best numbers we can, since the value of a vintage muscle car can often be directly related to the number that were produced.

The emphasis of this book is on the top-of-the-line versions of each model of car. It should be noted, however, that on certain occasions the high-performance powerplants could also be ordered in more basic models of the car. Special variations, such as those cars modified by factory-authorized companies or dealers, are also covered since their rarity makes them extremely valuable.

Unlike other automotive books, every photo in this book is of an actual, existing machine. These cars *do* exist, and they are appreciated and driven by owners who are still living the muscle car era.

So that's the scene, and this is admittedly a larger subject than can be completely covered by one volume. With that in mind, this book will broadly cover all the models of the cars that made up those wonderful high-performance years. After setting the scene in the first chapter, the next four chapters address the supercars of General Motors, Ford, Chrysler, and American Motors.

The book also addresses offshoots of the sport. Chapter 6 covers the low-number production high-performance factory drag and road-racing machines. These rare muscle cars have greatly increased in value, and many of them are participating today in exhibition and vintage racing events. Chapter 7 covers another interesting aspect of this sport with the low production and muscular Indy 500 Pace Car replicas that were (and are) produced each year for the big race. Their values are gaining at a rapid rate as the years go by. Both the factory racers and pace cars have been swept up by the muscle car craze.

Three appendices should help those interested in getting into the muscle car hobby. Listings provide the addresses of existing muscle car clubs, muscle car registries, and parts and accessory vendors.

With the wide range of muscle cars covered by this book, it's difficult to concentrate heavily on any particular model or brand. The emphasis again is on the high-performance versions of all the models. The purpose of this book, then, is to provide a "primer" on the collection and restoration hobby, which exploded in the 1980s and certainly shows no signs of backing off in the 1990s. What the last decade of this century will bring with these cars is anybody's guess.

So here they are: the American muscle cars.

CHAPTER 1

The Hows and Whys

MUSCLE IS AN INTERESTING WORD IN OUR LANGUAGE. IT CAN MEAN MANY DIF-ferent things. Webster defines the word as having to do with motion and strength, certainly two terms that are appropriate in describing the exciting high-performance American muscle cars of the 1960s and early 1970s.

The acquiring, restoring, driving, and exhibiting of these unique machines has become a regular part of the American love affair with the automobile. The neck-snapping power of these cars, along with their racy looks, have generated this amazing phenomenon as a whole new automotive cult has been born. As interest in these cars has continued to increase, their values have spiraled to amazing figures — $100,000 and much more in some cases.

THE MUSCLE CAR ERA

The early 1960s were really the beginning of the muscle car era as we know it, although there were a number of big-horsepower models being developed in the late 1950s. These cars, though, just don't seem to have the high interest factor today of their later brothers. Much of the popularity of these cars in the 1960s came from the involvement of the manufacturers in the building of factory drag and oval-track race cars. These specially modified cars brought exposure to their production-line brethren, and the exposure paid off. The old saying "Race on Sunday, sell on Monday" was often heard in those days. But just as the interest in musclebound machines got underway in the mid-1960s, it faded just as quickly in the early 1970s.

The 1950s starting point for the horsepower increases began when a number of powerplants exceeding 300 cubic inches were developed. In the early 1960s, the trend continued with the introduction of Chevy's twin-carbed 409;

shortly thereafter came Ford's 427-cubic-inch powerplants. Tables 1-1 and 1-2 show the growth trends in performance from the Big Three automakers in terms of cubic inches and horsepower. These tables clearly illustrate the 1950s roots, the rise during the 1960s, and the dropoff during the early 1970s.

Table 1-1. Top Horsepower Figures by Manufacturer, 1961-1971.

	General Motors	Ford	Chrysler
1961	315	360	330
1962	409	405	420
1963	425	425	425
1964	425	425	425
1965	425	425	425
1966	435	447	425
1967	435	425	425
1968	435	390	425
1969	430	335	425
1970	450	375	425
1971	425	375	425

Table 1-2. Top Musclecar Engine Size in Cubic Inches by Manufacturer, 1961-1971.

	General Motors	Ford	Chrysler
1961	389	390	413
1962	409	406	413
1963	409	427	426
1964	421	427	426
1965	421	427	426
1966	421	428	426
1967	428	428	440
1968	428	428	440
1969	455	429	440
1970	455	429	440
1971	455	351	440

A number of factors dropped the bottom out of the market for these big-power machines. The cost of insurance for these cars skyrocketed, and new government standards for emissions and bumper crashworthiness stripped them of much of their jolt. The first energy crisis of 1973 and 1974 was the final blow to all but a few high-performance lines (such as Pontiac's Trans Am).

Possibly the most important attribute a muscle car could have was performance at the dragstrip. A look at the test runs of some of the breed in their original treks down the strip shows which of them really were muscle cars. The figures show that the 1966 427 Cobra was the fastest of the lot, with a 118-mile-per-hour clocking in only 12.2 seconds for the quarter-mile distance. (Was that machine a passenger car or a race car?) Two Corvettes were in the top 10 with a 1966 (a *very* good year) 427 'Vette (112 mph in 12.8 seconds) and a 1968 model (108/13.3) in seventh place. Chrysler products showed well, with a 1969 Road Runner third (111.8/12.91), a 1970 Hemi 'Cuda in fourth (107.12/13.1), a 1970 Hemi Road Runner in eighth (107.5/13.34), and a 1969 Hemi Charger in tenth (109/13.48).

General Motors picked up the remainder of the dragstrip top 10 with a 1970 454 Chevelle in fifth (107.01/13.12), a 1969 ZL1 Camaro (110.21/13.16) in seventh, and a 1970 Buick GS Stage I coming in ninth (105.5/13.38). The first Ford product on the list after the Cobra was a 1969 Boss 429 Mustang in 14th place (106/13.6). Once again, all these figures must be taken with a grain of salt, but rest assured that these are all genuine high-performance machines, and if you are fortunate enough to own one of them, you are a *very* lucky individual.

OWNING A MUSCLE CAR

With the ever-increasing value of muscle machines, the current muscle car owner is faced with a dilemma: Has the car suddenly become too valuable to drive, to say nothing of actually *racing* it? To many owners, the thrill of owning these cars is being able to punch that accelerator to the floor and bring those ponies under the hood to life. But the chance of dropping transmission parts on the pavement or breaking a rod in a valuable power train prompts second thoughts.

Other owners have effectively retired the cars safely under tarps in the garage, getting them out only for that occasional Sunday drive or to show them off at a car show. Still others look at the cars primarily as a way to make money. The most desirable of the vintage muscle cars were produced in extremely low numbers, often in the mere hundreds or fewer. Restoring these cars for investment purposes is, according to one muscle car expert, "Better than diamonds." Should this hoarding practice continue to grow, all the desirable cars will be gone from the hobby in a few more years.

I'm sad to have to announce that not all is squeaky-clean in this automotive hobby. To be blunt about it, the big-money aspect of the sport has produced cheating. This usually involves taking a particular car and changing the sheet metal, engine, emblems, or other hardware, representing it as something it's not. Some models are ridiculously easy to re-create. With the availability of reproduction parts and pieces, the job is even easier. This dishonest practice will continue to grow in the 1990s, so the buyer should beware when looking for a dream machine. Make sure you get exactly what you think you are paying for.

The muscle car craze has actually advanced to the point that dealers search out, restore, and wheel-and-deal the high-performance models. Want a 409 Chevy or a Super Cobra Jet Torino? These guys can find it for you — at a price, of course!

Granted, enthusiasts of all ages and income levels are involved in this hobby, but one age group in particular seems to constitute the largest percentage of the craze. The current "fortysomething" age group was young when these cars were new, and many of them have harbored dreams of owning one since their youth. These are the cars they couldn't afford then, but they're now ready and able to plunk down many times the original retail price for that Hemi 'Cuda or SS396 Chevelle.

The search is on in this country to find the last of these unique performance machines. Stories still surface about rare cars being found in barns or being purchased at rock-bottom prices from unknowing sellers. Then there's the dream that in some out-of-the way junkyard one of these cars is buried under a stack of junkers, just waiting to be discovered. They have been found in the past, but those days are rapidly fading away.

Surprisingly, though, a large number of the more heavily produced muscle cars are still around, and many can be purchased for reasonable prices, if you're ready to undertake an often massive restoration effort. Many such cars can be seen plying the streets of America in the hands of teenagers. These cars are usually modified and more often than not also carry liberal dose of rust. With their value continuing to increase, however, the time will surely come when even some of these basket cases will be bought and restored.

RESTORATION

The level of restoration on some rare muscle cars is truly amazing and can run to staggering sums. Many such cars were once rusted-out hulks, outwardly appearing worthless. However, the VIN (Vehicle Identification Number) plate on a car can make a complete rebuild worth the money. One owner laughingly related that about the only original piece left after his restoration was that VIN plate — practically everything else was new! Such restorations can cost tens of thousands of dollars, but the finished product can be worth as much as six figures.

The term restoration has also taken on new meaning in the muscle car arena. For the purist, everything on the car must be stock, and exactly the way it came from the factory. Arguments are heard at times about the correct color shade of the engine block, or whether the engine is carrying the correctly dated carburetor. Many times, factory data is not available to verify a particular option. Another factor that often creates confusion is when a car is equipped with what appears to be a non-stock item that the original owner swears was on the car when he bought it new. This situation occurs because the manufacturers sometimes used off-brand vendors near the end of a production run. It certainly presents problems to car show judges when these items appear.

Precise reproduction of factory equipment is some muscle car owners' game, but for others, the fun is in the jolting performance of the cars. Many of these cars have slight—and sometimes not-so-slight—changes in both power-plant and appearance, including aftermarket wheels, altered paint schemes, and bumper-to-bumper chrome. On occasion, engines carrying tunnel-ram carburetion systems or even superchargers can be seen popping through the hood!

Again, with the value of these cars ever-escalating, many of them are being converted back to their stock configuration.

MUSCLE CAR CLUBS

The increasing popularity of the muscle car hobby can be measured by the ever-growing sizes of the many national muscle car clubs. Many such clubs hold national meets, some including actual drag racing where the owners can risk the innards of their valuable machines on the track. A surprising number of owners accept the challenge—and the risk.

Another growing phenomenon is the increasing number of muscle car "registries." These are private-party (usually the owner of a particular model who wants to communicate with other similar owners) undertakings in which the number of a particular model still in existence is sought. Such individuals often spread the word in the muscle car magazines for owners to send in the information and particulars on their machines.

Speaking of muscle car magazines, their numbers have grown in the 1980s with the rest of the hobby. The major magazines include *Musclecar Review*, *Muscle Cars*, *Guide to Muscle Cars*, *Musclecar Classics*, *Cars and Parts Muscle Cars*, and others. In addition, many of the "other" car magazines also cover the muscle car scene. There's an explosion of information on the subject. In fact, it's usually easier to find reference data on these cars today than it was when they were new.

Even the model manufacturers have gotten into the game. Along with the modern factory and race cars that sit on the hobby shop racks, there is an increasing number of vintage muscle car kits—and they have been selling well. In another merchandising area, fans of a particular car can often be seen wearing T-shirts and hats carrying pictures of their particular muscle cars.

They are everywhere you look, these American muscle cars.

CHAPTER II

General Motors Muscle Cars

GENERAL MOTORS WAS A MAJOR PLAYER IN THE MUSCLE GAME DURING THE golden years of power and performance. Four of the five GM divisions were involved, and each division operated separately, so the cars were not mirror images of each other; each division had its own personality and unique power plants.

Those were exciting times, with new models and power trains being developed and announced at regular intervals. Even staid Buick sported its Gran Sport and GSX models, two performance machines that deviated from that division's luxury and family car image. Impressive 455-cubic inch powerplants provided the performance for these machines on the street and strip.

Chevrolet's Camaro line, introduced in 1967 to counter Ford's successful Mustang, was a popular muscle machine. It was honored twice during the 1960s as the Indy Pace Car. Flashy styling with 302, 396, and even 427 engines stuffed under the hood made the Camaro a real killer, and the aluminum-block 427 ZL1 Camaro is a muscle collectible of the highest order for the 1990s.

The Super Sport Chevelle was a favorite with the young set during the late 1960s and represents a valuable collectible today. The SS396 and SS454 models could get it on with the best and either makes an excellent choice for restoration. The Chevelle's truck variant, the sporty El Camino, also represents an interesting muscle vehicle and a scramble is on to find the big-engine models. The "luxury performance" Monte Carlo and the economical Nova were similarly endowed motorwise.

Already a true sports car, the Corvette benefited in a big way during the muscle rage with huge powerplants and light weight. The 'Vette was a raging performer with the 396, 427, and 454-cubic inch powerplants. With these engines, some vintage Corvettes are reaching astronomical six-figure values and should continue that growth trend in the years to come.

One of the most famous engines ever built by General Motors was the powerful 409-cubic inch Chevrolet. Honored in song, the engine was available in a number of models and showed its dominance on the nation's dragstrips. The 409-powered cars are drawing huge prices, even for those of the Plain Jane variety.

Oldsmobile competed in the muscle wars with a number of impressive big- and small-block engines. The 4-4-2 and famous W machines carried powerplants of up to 455 cubic inches and the cars are receiving increasing interest among collectors.

Finally, the Pontiac lineup featured a number of muscle offerings during the period. In the pony car area, the Firebird and its upscale Trans Am line featured powerplants of 400 and 455 cubic inches.

In the intermediate Pontiac line, the GTO, Judge, and T-37 models benefited performance-wise from 389, 428, and 455-cubic-inch power plants. A number of other Pontiac models also benefited from the use of an impressive 421-cubic inch engine.

General Motors played the muscle car game in a big way, and its accomplishments are remembered today by the escalating price tags on some of its creations of that wonderful era of performance and power.

BUICK DIVISION

Buick's stodgy and conservative image was tough to shake. After all, the division's very name conjures up visions of heavy four-door luxury-barges. Buick meant family cars, stability, and success in business. Despite its image, Buick did manage to bolt together a couple of world-beaters during the muscle era. In fact, the sports-oriented GSX was one of the fastest muscle cars of its time. From a value viewpoint in today's market, one of these old "family cars" might be a great place to invest your money. Don't wait too long, though, because the word is getting out on Buick.

Skylark Gran Sport

Like many General Motors muscle cars, the Gran Sport (GS) began life as an option on another model, in this case the Skylark. The Skylark Gran Sport, as it was known, carried the 401-cubic-inch, 325-hp power plant. Identification of this initial (1965) GS was accomplished with Gran Sport emblems on the roof, grille, and deck.

The GS looked a lot more like a muscle car the following year, through the addition of a number of flashy appearance options, giving the car the look to go with its high-horsepower engine. The hood ornament was shaved off the hood (whoever heard of a muscle car with a hood ornament?) and other appearance changes included fake air scoops, a blacked-out grille, standard 7.75 × 14 tires, and side striping. The GS was maturing fast.

Two versions of the GS appeared on the marque for 1967. The 400-cubic-inch version remained, although the horsepower figure was now boosted to 340.

Dubbed the Skylark GS-400, the model featured a pair of hood scoops, a new grille design, and striping. The GS name was also tagged to a lower-powered version, the GS-340, which carried a 340-cubic-inch, 220-hp powerplant, hardly a machine that should carry a muscle connotation.

GS 350, GS 400, GS 455

In 1968, the model's recognition was solidified with the dropping of the Skylark name for the GS — and the hyphen from the nameplate. It would, however, still be possible to order the later Skylarks with the big 400 and 455 powerplants, making them genuine — although not well-recognized — muscle cars. The 1968 models were known simply as the GS 350 and the GS 400. No longer the little-boy-lost, the 350 had picked up 60 additional horses under the hood and the model had the new looks on the outside to go with the power. Nonfunctional intakes on the front quarters, a new accent stripe and grille treatment, and other interior appointments made the GS 350 stand out in a crowd. Although not as popular as its big-block brothers, the GS 350 will almost certainly increase in popularity as the GS 400s are grabbed up. (A number of the GS 350s should still be out there, as 8,317 were produced.)

A total of 13,197 lightly updated GS 400s rolled off the production line that year. Carrying the same 340-hp powerplant, the 400 sported new vents in the front quarters, twin functional hood scoops, and a chromed air cleaner top.

But the GS 400 also had a very interesting performance option called the "Stage One Special Package," a dealer-installed powerplant for drag-strip operation. The engine was quoted as having only a five-horsepower increase over the stock GS 400 engine, but that was a joke and everybody knew it, because this engine was worth at least a 10 to 15 percent increase in power. The new engine carried advanced valve springs, forged pistons, and an 11:1 compression ratio. In testing, the new powerplant was worth about six miles per hour over the standard GS on the drag strip.

Induction was the key word for 1969. Every GS engine carried the $199 Stage One package. Here's how it worked: The twin hood-mounted scoops fed the air into a special air cleaner. Twin snorkels on the air cleaner made a firm connection when the hood was closed. The engine was effectively fed with cool outside air as compared with the normal hot engine air. The increase in engine performance was sizable.

Other components included in the Stage One package included a special camshaft, a dual exhaust system, an upgraded oiling system, and a heavy-duty cooling package. Other available options could turn your GS 400 into an excellent road machine. Among them were a 15:1 power steering unit and a Rallye Ride Control package.

For 1970, the Gran Sport kicked off the new decade in style with a brand-new big-block 455-cubic-inch powerplant. The old Buick image was definitely changing in a big way. The reliable old 400 engine was gone after a long and successful tenure.

The Buicks were completely restyled for 1970 and they were knockouts. Tim Stockine makes use of his '70 Buick GS Stage 1's horsepower by occasionally running the car at the dragstrip.

Two versions of the 455 were available: the 455 Stage 1 version, which was rated at 360 horses, and the more sedate GS 455 engine, rated at just 10 horses less. The torque listed for both versions was a ground-pounding 510 foot-pounds. The 455s were basically bored-out 400s with a .2725-inch increase in bore but no change in stroke. Internals for the engines included forged rods, aluminum pistons, and an iron crank. Compression ratio was 10:1 for both models. The previous year's 350-cubic-inch 315-hp engine was also still available.

The Buick performance machines also had a new look for 1970 to go along with their new powerplants. They sure didn't look like the old family car anymore. Both the GS 455 and Stage One models had their own 455 identifiers, with a GS 455 emblem appearing on the blacked-out grille and the front fenders and a GS on the trunk lid. For the Stage One, Stage One emblems replaced the 455 emblems. A total of 10,148 were produced, with only 1,416 convertibles, making those ragtops very desirable.

For 1971, the 455 engine stayed around, but the former GS 400 and Stage One engines were combined into a single 455 engine. The cubic inches were there, but the horsepower figures were on a downward trend, and the 455 engine for 1971 was rated at only 315 horsepower. The compression ratio was degraded by 15 percent, which was the main reason for the power reduction. The GS versions were powered by the 350-cube power plant, now rated at 260 horses.

Even though the power was down under the hood, the racy looks topside were retained. Included were bright rocker panel moldings, blacked-out grilles,

Buick's 455-cubic-inch powerplant, capable of 360 horses, was new for 1970.

still-functional scoops, and flashy trim. The GS and GS 455 emblems were utilized to identify the particular model. Production for both models was slightly down, with 8,268 hardtops and 902 convertibles built.

The Gran Sport's last true year was 1972, and it was just a mere shadow of its former muscular self. Two models were available, the GS 350 and GS 455. The horsepower downturn trend was in high gear with the 350's power falling like a rock to only 175 net hp, while the once-mighty 455 had shrunk to a mere 225. Muscle car powerplants? Hardly, even though the muscular appearance had been maintained. The final production figures were 7,723 hardtops and 852 convertibles. The GS nomenclature was actually carried through 1975 as an option.

As the 1990s get under way, the popularity of these lower horsepower early-'70s Buicks is at a low level. However, as the availability of the late '60s Gran Sports dries up, it is likely that these cars will generate new interest among muscle hobbyists.

GSX

Just when you thought that the GS 455 Stage One was the ultimate Buick muscle machine, along came the GSX in 1970. Not much is different between the two cars, but the look of the GSX sets it apart. The engines for this special edition model were identical to the 455 and Stage One powerplants available for the

The 1970 and 1971 GSX models were really nothing more than decked-out GS Stage Is. Flashy looks and body-length striping make the GSX the most desirable of early Buick muscle.

1970 Gran Sport, with a majority of the GSXs being built with the Stage One variant. A total of only 678 GSXs were constructed that model year, the only year the GSX was built as a recognized model.

One thing about the GSX — you couldn't miss it when you saw it. The GSX was available in only two colors, Apollo White or a bright Saturn Yellow, which was about as yellow as you can get. Then there were the graphics: twin wide black stripes that outlined the twin hood scoops, and a long stripe that streaked down the body side and kicked up on the rear quarter to run across the rear spoiler. Finally, there was a blacked-out grille and black front spoiler. The two-color GSX emblem identified this rare breed on the grille, rear fenders, and in the middle of the rear of the spoiler.

Buick touted the GSX as a way of customizing your Gran Sport with all the different appearance options that were available. Granted, it was really nothing more than a spruced up Gran Sport with exactly the same power trains and performance, but because of its out-of-sight looks and extremely low production, the GSX is one hot ticket for the 1990s. If you have a chance to buy one, grab it in a hurry.

The GSX was dropped to a special option in 1971, the last time the famous three-letter initials would be seen. Only 124 were produced that year, making it a super-rare machine. The 345-hp version of the 455 was the standard power-plant. Externally, the 1971 GSX looked almost identical to the 1970 model.

The GSX's 455-cubic-inch engine gulped cold, fresh air from special hood ducting.

CHEVROLET DIVISION

Everybody in the American automotive industry knew that it had to come. General Motors had to respond to the super-successful Ford Mustang, introduced in 1964. The bet was also solid that whatever the response would be, there would be a muscular angle to the new GM machine. Rumors had been circulating since shortly after the Mustang's introduction, and finally, early in 1966, General Motors let the cat out of the bag and indicated that its answer to the Mustang would be the Chevrolet Camaro, with a fall 1966 release date. Camaro engine options would range from in-line six-cylinders to heavy-hitting big-blocks. Through its muscle years, the Camaro was available in a number of different models including the Super Sport, Z/28, and the famous COPO machines.

Camaro Super Sports

Chevrolet used extensive computer analysis to come up with the initial sleek design for the Camaro. Appearance and performance options abounded on the new model, making it an immediate success with the public.

The standard powerplant for the 1967 Super Sport option was the 350-cubic-inch engine, which evolved from boring out Chevy's venerable 327. One hot street and strip performer, the 350 was capable of an impressive 295 horsepower, which certainly put it in the muscle category. The new 350 featured a 10:1 compression ratio, large valves, and a four-inch bore.

Along with the 295-hp engine on the 1967 Camaro SS350 came front nose stripes, sport suspension, SS emblems, redline tires, and an imitation-grilled hood. The SS package grabbed the sport crowd immediately, and 29,270 were sold that first year.

To add a little confusion to the optioning of the Camaro, a Rally Sport (RS) option was also available. Included in this appearance group were concealed headlights, relocated parking and backup lights, larger taillight lenses, special body striping, and wheelhouse moldings. RS and SS packages could be ordered together or separately. When used with the SS package, the RS identifier was superceded by the SS badging, but when used alone, the car carried RS emblems.

Of interest—great interest to be sure—to the performance-minded was the introduction later in the model year of the 396-cubic-inch powerplant for the Camaro. Only 4,003 of the big-block models were sold, but rest assured that those SS396 Camaros are highly sought after today. The initial 396s (the L35s) had an advertised horsepower rating of 325, but there was more to come. Later in the year, even more power would hit the street in the form of the L78 version of the 396, which was capable of an additional 50 horses. Only 1,138 of this most desirable model were built.

Camaro Super Sports could also be ordered with the Rally Sport trim package, as shown on this '67 RS/SS convertible. When both packages were ordered together, the SS badging took precedence.

The base 325-hp powerplant of an early SS396 Camaro.

For 1968, the Camaro's engine options remained very similar to the first year's, except for the introduction of two more versions of the 396 engine. The L34 version was capable of 350 horses and 2,579 were sold. The L89 version, of which only 272 were sold, added aluminum heads for the ultimate performance. A number of these cars have been located, but they are very rare—and very expensive! The 325-hp version, however, remains the most accessible of the big-block Camaros, with 10,773 being sold that second model year; L78 production would vault to a 4,575 units in 1968.

A number of minor changes marked the '68 Camaros, with a new interior console, a redesigned grille, and suspension changes for the bigger-engine packages. For the 350- and 396-powered models, multileaf springs and staggered shocks were added.

The next year, 1969, was another good one for big-block Camaros. Production figures show that the best-seller of the 396 engines was the 325-hp version, with 6,752 built. The powerful 375-hp L78 was second at 4,889, with the L34 bringing up the rear with 2,018 sold.

The Camaro was all-new for 1970 from both performance and appearance viewpoints. It was as though the SS had turned away from its muscle car image to more of a sports-car outlook. Engine choices were reduced, with the standard powerplant for the SS being the Turbo-Fire 350-cubic inch, 300-hp engine. The L34 and L78 big-blocks were optional, but the purchasing fire had burned out with only 1,864 and 600 cars, respectively, carrying these powerplants.

The legendary L78 375-hp 396. If the air cleaner decal was missing, the L78 could be distinguished by its aluminum intake manifold and Holley carb.

The brand-new Camaro SS package for the first year of the new decade included a full-width bumper with blacked-out grille, rear edge molding on the hood, and numerous SS emblems. As always, the ever-important engine displacement was carried on the front fenders. The F41 suspension option was available on any '70 SS. There were also special appearance options under the hood, with aluminum valve covers for the 350 engines and chrome covers for the 396s. The SS396s also carried heavier motor mounts and special suspension modifications.

Appearance-wise, the 1971 Camaro looked virtually identical to the 1970, but the horses under the hood were running away as the Camaro's muscle car image began to fade. The only big-block offered was the 300-hp LS3 396; only 1,533 of these were built.

Things got even worse in 1972, the last year for the Super Sport and the lowest year of production for the Camaro. The 396 engine was still around, but just barely. A drop of 60 horses in 1972 left the 396 beating out only 240 horses. The 350 small-block was the only other option for the year.

The SS396 Camaros remain as highly collectible machines for the 1990s, with an unlimited potential for value growth. As the 396 car numbers continue to decrease, though, the SS350s will undoubtedly become more and more desirable to muscle car collectors.

Camaro Z/28

The Super Sport wasn't the only hot Camaro to debut in 1967. The limited-production Z/28, the dream of design genius Vince Piggins, was built to qualify the model for Trans Am racing, and the Camaro that evolved looked and acted like a real racing machine.

A unique powerplant was designed and built for the Z/28 based on the long-standing 327-cubic-inch small-block. The engine was destroked to 302 cubic inches and provided with a forged-steel crankshaft. With an 11:1 compression ratio and a monstrous Holley 800 CFM carb, the 302 was a real screamer! General Motors literature rated the 302's horsepower at 290, a figure that seems extremely low after taking a ride in this rocket.

It was possible to get one of three Z/28 performance packages that first year; these ranged in price from $437 to $858. A number of performance items were available, including headers and a cold-air induction system. This first Z/28 is the rarest of all the Zs, with an extremely low production total of 602. Valuable? Rare? Desirable? Easy to fake? All of the above!

The popularity of the initial Z/28 saw its 1968 production total move up more than tenfold to 7,199. The changes to the little performance machine were minimal, with only slight internal changes made to the 302 powerplant. The value of the Z/28 continues to increase in today's muscle car market even though it doesn't carry a big-block engine. Most collectors still consider the Z/28 a

This 1968 version of the Z/28 302 had rare dual carbs. Note air cleaner ducting to cowl area.

The 1969 Z/28 302 dual carb setup was sealed to the special ZL2 cowl induction hood.

The more commonly seen standard Z/28 engine with one four-barrel carb.

The 1969 Z/28's 290 horses and flashy design have made it a very desirable collectible for the 1990s. This car also carries the Rally Sport option.

A new powerplant for the Z/28 appeared in 1970 with the super-hot 350-cubic-inch, 360-horse-plant LT-1.

muscle car of the first order. The Z love affair continued through 1969 with 20,302 sold.

For 1970, the high-revving 302 engine was gone, replaced by a 350-cubic inch, 360-hp ticket referred to as the LT1; 8,733 of the model were sold. A year later, the same cubic inches were in place but the horsepower dropped by 30. There was also a ton of high-performance equipment available with the model including a Positraction rear axle, heavy-duty cooling system, and dual exhausts. Racy looks were not forgotten; a blacked-out grille, hood and rear deck stripes, and wheel trim rings were included. But like the other General Motors muscle cars, the LT1 was the beginning of the end of the performance era and production trailed off to about half that of the previous year, with only 4,862 coming down the line. The downward trend for the once-great Z continued in 1972, with only 2,575 produced.

COPO Camaros

The horsepower wars were at their peak in 1969 and Chevy had its own weapon. It was called the COPO (Central Office Production Order) Camaro and came in both iron- and aluminum-block versions of the 427-cubic inch powerplant.

The COPO 9561 iron-block version was rated at a ground-pounding 425 horses, while the COPO 9560 ZL1 aluminum-engined cars rated an additional five horses. The numbers of these exotically powered Camaros built were miniscule to say the least. Exactly 69 of the ZL1 Camaros were built, but to this day no one knows for sure how many of the L72 iron-block 427 Camaros were built

The tipoff that this car is one of the legendary COPO Camaros is the ZL2 cowl induction hood on a Plain-Jane Camaro — the ZL2 was only available on Z/28 and SS models, and was standard on COPOs. This one is a rare aluminum-engined ZL1 owned by Cliff Ernst of Tennessee. Contrary to popular belief, the COPO Camaros did not come standard with Rally Wheels or D80 front and rear spoilers — they were available as extra-cost options.

under COPO 9561. It *is* known that 1,015 L72 engines coded specifically for this application were produced, but this number also includes service and warranty replacement units, so your guess as to the number of COPO 9561s is probably as good as anybody else's.

These powerful cars were mainly sold to dealerships for racing. Even before the mighty COPOs became available in early 1969, however, a number of Chevrolet dealers, including Baldwin/Motion in Baldwin, New York; Dana in California; Nickey in Chicago; and Yenko in Canonsburg, Pennsylvania, had been building their own 427 Camaro conversions as far back as 1967. These conversions usually started out as SS396s and were then modified with 427 powerplants (short-blocks only or complete engines) and suspension and handling modifications. A number of these rare conversions have been located and restored. It goes without saying that their values could reach well into the six-figure category.

The Yenko is the best known of these conversions, and it is well-documented that Yenko purchased about 200 of the 1969 COPO 9561 cars and converted them into Yenko SC Camaros (published Yenko figures include 198, 199, and 201; the latter is currently the most widely accepted number). Yenko made no changes to the existing L72 power trains, just cosmetic enhancements. The Yenkos carried the cowl-induction ZL2 hood (as did all COPO Camaros), rear spoiler, and front air dam, along with other accessories. All Yenkos were "double COPOs," in fact, coming equipped with the COPO 9737 sports car conversion package that turned them, for all practical purposes, into big-block Z/28s. The cars, though, were best identified by their distinctive Yenko striping, which consisted of twin stripes on the hood terminating in an "arrowhead" with

The 1969 Yenko SC Camaro was converted by the Yenko dealership but the COPO 9561 L72 427 engine was retained. Earlier versions of the 427 Yenko (1967, 1968) had their 396 engines replaced with the 427 powerplants.

This 425-hp, 427-cubic-inch L72 is stuffed into a COPO 9561 Camaro, this one a Yenko SYC. Yenko decaled its engines with 450 HP; standard L72s wore 425 HP stickers.

SYC lettering. Another stripe swept down each side of the car with YENKO/SC lettering on the rear fender; several Yenko badges were also included.

Chevelle Super Sports

When the horsepower race heated up in the early 1960s, Chevy realized that to remain in the game it would have to punch up its Chevelle line. The other divisions of General Motors were kicking up the cubic inches—not to mention what the opposition was doing.

Chevrolet's Chevelle, with its famous Super Sport option, was one macho-looking machine in 1964. The performance image of the model was certainly there with options such as a tach, sport steering wheel, chrome trim items, and gauges—a tough-looking machine to be sure, but without much power under the hood. The best that could be acquired was a 283-cubic-inch engine providing a disappointing 195 horses.

Even the midyear introduction of the 327 engine didn't solve the horsepower image problem that the Chevelle faced. The power figure was now a respectable 300 horses, with a 250-hp version also available, but those powerplants were still a far cry from the big-blocks that were now in the showrooms of the enemy camps.

Then, in 1965, it happened. The Chevelle's magic numbers suddenly became 396 and 375 — cubic inches and horsepower, respectively. Characteristics of the magnificent new motor included a forged crank, cast-iron heads, and an 800 CFM Holley Carb, all decked out in a neatly detailed machine.

The new heavy-hauler Chevelle would be called the Z16, but the numbers produced that first year would be minimal — only 201 cars, to be exact. But the Z16 option (which carried a sizable $1,501 price tag) meant a lot more than just the 396 under the hood.

A number of significant modifications were made to the Chevelle's body in the Z16 buildup. First, in order to accept the increased power and torque of the new engine, the frame was beefed up, and a stronger suspension with new stabilizer bars was added. Other modifications included full-size 11-inch brakes, quicker steering, and special heavy-duty shocks and springs.

The 1965 Z16s were built on the vintage boxy Malibu bodies, the last year that style would be used. The model was identified low on the rear deck lid with "Malibu SS396" with the 396 numbers blocked out in red. Very few of these first-of-their-kind Super Sports have so far been located and each can be considered a treasure. The Z16, though, was just the beginning of an exciting era of big-block Chevy performance. This first SS396 Chevelle was a great public relations coup, and would serve to introduce the brutish Chevelles that would follow in the remainder of the decade.

The 396-powered Chevelle was a much more streetable vehicle for 1966, with much of the Z16 high-performance driving option mellowed. The standard 396 was now rated at 325 horses, although, with the addition of a special cam, the horsepower figure jumped to 360 in the L34 version. The L78 375-hp version was also offered near the end of the model year.

The Z-16 was the first Chevelle to answer the muscle car call. The 396 engine produced 375 horses for the Malibu-based body. The machines were produced in limited numbers, only 201, and few have been located. Here's one of the best, a 1990 restoration by Harold Vieth of Iowa.

A rare sight — a 375-hp L78-396 in a 1965 216 Chevelle.

Now called the SS396, the top Chevelle model for 1966 featured simulated hood intakes, vinyl interiors, Super Sport script lettering on the rear quarter, and SS 396 emblems. In a great year for Chevy, the 396 Chevelle sold an impressive 72,272 units in convertible and hardtop styles.

The Chevelle saw few changes in the engine compartment for 1967, with the standard 325 and 375-horsepower engine ratings remaining. The 360-horsepower engine figure, though, would be reduced by 10 in the L34 model. The SS396 featured a blacked-out grille with SS396 tag and other appearance options. SS396 production was slightly down from 1966, with 63,006 rolling off the line.

A complete body restyling was the keynote for the Chevelle Super Sport in 1968. This new Super Sport was a real looker, with a slightly smaller body than the previous year.

The 325-horse powerplant was again the standard big-block for the SS396 in 1968, with the L34 350-hp and L78 375-hp versions listed as options at $105 and $237, respectively. Of the 57,600 Chevelle SS396s sold during that model year, fewer than 2,000 carried the L78 engine. Needless to say, those machines are highly sought after by collectors these days.

Slight appearance changes were accomplished on the '69 Super Sport, with the big-block engine offerings remaining basically unchanged. However, for those who weren't quite up to driving the 396 power plants, a new 350-cubic inch, 300-hp engine designated the L48 was available for an additional outlay of $48.

The 1969 Super Sport Chevelle carried a 396 powerplant, which was discontinued after 1970.

If you knew a magic number—9562—you could get a 425-hp L72 427-incher in your '69 Chevelle. You see, 9562 was the COPO (Central Office Production Order) number of the only 427 Chevelles ever built, and, just as was the case with the COPO Camaros, a lucky few in the know would drive off the showroom floor in the very same dream supercars that were being hand-built with sweat and dollars in garages all across America. To this day, it's not known exactly how many 427 Chevelles were actually built in 1969 (their very existence was rumored and disputed for years), but it is now known that Chevrolet produced 358 complete L72 engines coded specifically for this application. That number includes projected service and warranty needs, so the number of cars built must be something under 358. The experts are still trying to pin the exact number down at this writing, and we may never know for sure.

Take a good look—this might be the only 1969 COPO 9562 427 Chevelle you ever see. Externally, these super-rare machines looked identical to SS396 Chevelles, but without any SS or 396 badging or emblems. (Basic Malibus carried more chrome trim.)

It does seem certain, however, that something like 100 (99 is the most often quoted number) of the 427 Chevelles went to Yenko Chevrolet in Canonsburg, Pennsylvania, for conversion into Yenko SC Chevelles. As with the more famous Yenko SC Camaros, Yenko left the 425-hp L72 engines alone (except for possibly adding tube headers) and concentrated on the appearance of the machines, adding trademark graphic striping, SYC headrests, and Yenko badges. One appearance anomaly on the Yenko SC Chevelles was the presence of Rally wheels instead of the SS Chevelle's usual Super Sport wheels (the COPO Chevelles were identical to SS396 models in appearance except for the complete absence of SS and SS396 emblems, and thus should have come through with the SS wheels). The reason for this is that the Yenko Chevelles were also outfitted with the COPO 9737 Sports Car Conversion package—the same type of setup installed on all SC Camaros—which featured the 15-inch Rallys instead of the 14-inch SS wheels. At this writing, only about 35 of the rare Yenko Chevelles have so far been located.

Getting back to the regular production machines, many Chevelle musclecar fans consider the 1970 model to be the best and most desirable of the breed. That opinion relates directly to the introduction of the bone-jarring LS6 454-cubic inch, 450-horsepower engine. The new engine came as a part of the SS454 option, which listed at $263, and those extra 58-cubic-inches could really blow away the 396 machines on the dragstrip.

To produce its breathtaking power, the LS6 used 11.25:1 compression heads, a special solid lifter cam, aluminum intake, forged crank, and a giant 780 CFM Holley carb. This was one powerplant that was definitely ready to stand on its own against the opposition, an easy 13-second dragstrip performer.

But there were also lesser power options for 1970. An LS5 version of the 454 was worth 360 horsepower, while two potent 396 engines produced 350 in the

Don Yenko took delivery of 99 rare COPO 9562 427 Chevelles and gave them his SC dress-up treatment. This one wears Yenko/Atlas mag wheels; standard were Chevy Rally wheels, which replaced the factory Super Sport wheels on Yenko Chevelles with the COPO 9737 Sports Car Conversion. This beautiful rarity is owned by George Lyons of Pennsylvania.

The first year for the powerful 454-cubic-inch powerplant in the Chevelle was 1970. The LS6 version of this engine was worth 450 horses, with 13-second performance in the quarter mile.

L34 engine and 375 horsepower in the L78 version. The 396 engines were, from 1970 on, actually 402 cubic inches in displacement, but because of the popularity of the 396 number, the 396 designation remained. All 1970 Chevelle SS models will become more and more desirable in the 1990s, though the LS6 will continue to draw top dollar.

Even as pressure to stop building the big-block engines emerged in 1971, the popularity of the SS454s continued, with 19,992 sold. Both LS6 and LS5 powerplants remained available, with 425 and 365-hp ratings, respectively, for that year. The old reliable 396 was omitted from the lineup; two 350 engines filled the void, the L48 engine rated at 270 horses and the L65 at 25 hp less.

The 396 (the LS3 version) came back for a final bow in 1972, but it was a weak imitation of its tire-smoking brothers of the late 1960s. Its net horsepower was only 240. A watered-down version of the LS5 454 was only capable of 270 horses, while the once-potent 350 engines were now rated at 175 horses in the L48 and 165 in the L65 version.

The Chevelle line moved further and further away from its muscle car image as the 1970s continued—a sad time indeed for the performance-minded. By 1973, the 454 would make its final bow, rating only 245 net horsepower in its LS4 option, a far cry from its 450-hp rating in 1970.

It was the end of an era of great performance machines bearing the Chevelle name. The big-block 396s and 454s today rate among the most desirable muscle cars. Production figures of these cars was high enough that they are still available in adequate numbers. Get out there and get one before they're gone!

Corvette

The Corvette name means different things to different people. The Corvette is that expensive sports car you always wanted but could never afford. It's the sign of success in business, the car that says you've made it in the world. It's also synonymous with power and performance, with screaming engines pushing the small machines to magnificent acceleration and speeds.

For many enthusiasts, though, the Corvette presents somewhat of an enigma when it's referred to as a muscle car. Its sport car roots date back to its introduction in 1953, when the car was built with relatively small engines. That all changed in the 1960s, however, when the Corvette was equipped with some of the auto industry's largest and most powerful engines, making it one of the top performers on the muscle car list.

For muscle car collectors, big-engine 'Vettes are *the* hot ticket for the 1990s. During the late 1980s, it wasn't uncommon for a late-'60s big-block 'Vette to bring six figures, especially a low-production model.

The Corvette's muscle heritage can be traced back to the 1957 debut of its fuel-injected 283 V8, advertised at one horsepower per cubic inch. This produced some pretty healthy performance in a machine that weighed only 2730 pounds. The '57 Corvette was available with a positive traction rear axle and heavy-duty racing suspension, making it a real "mini" muscle car.

The dual-carb versions of the 283 boasted horsepower ratings of 245 and .270 in 1958. The 1958 fuel-injected version of the engine was capable of 290 horses. By 1960, the largest fuel-injected 283 had moved up to an impressive 315-horsepower rating. That high-performance option cost a hefty (for the time) $484. The dual-carb 283 rated 275 horses in 1961.

The next year, 1962, was a significant one for Corvette with the introduction of the 327-cubic-inch powerplant. The top fuel-injected version demonstrated an impressive 360 horsepower, while the two dual-carb versions were rated at 300 and 340 horsepower. In order to handle the impressive power, a number of

One of the most popular Corvettes ever built, this 1963 327-cubic-inch-powered model is reaching extremely high values. This marvelous example is owned by Scott McKee of Ohio.

performance options were also available, including heavy-duty brakes and a special suspension system.

The use of the familiar General Motors "L" engine designations began in 1963 with the L75 327-cubic-inch 300-horsepower engine, the L76 327/340, and the L84 327/360. The first two used a single four-barrel while the third still maintained its fuel-injection system. In 1964, the L84 power rating jumped to 375 horsepower.

The final year for the L84 was 1965, with the cost of the setup—$585—being the main reason for its demise. For comparison, the L76 single four-barrel engine that year could be ordered for only $129 extra for its 365 horsepower; the cost for the L84's extra 10 horses thus figured out to $411. Even so, the L84 was a superb engineering accomplishment, producing over one horsepower per cubic inch. The L84 featured special injection cylinder heads and an extremely high 11:1 compression ratio, which was consistent with the optimum operation of the fuel-injection system.

The end of the L84 was effectively accomplished by the new L78 396-cubic-inch, 425-horsepower engine. Although the 396-cubic-inch power plants would prove popular for several years in other Chevy products, the L78 396 would be only a one-year deal for the Corvette. This was the first 'Vette power plant to produce over 400 horsepower, but there were even bigger and better things to

This L36 390-hp version of the 427 resides in a Sting Ray. Note the special cover over the distributor to reduce radio interference in the fiberglass-bodied Corvette.

come. Only 2,157 L78s were sold in 1965, still more than the 771 L84-powered machines.

A number of changes were made to the '65 'Vette in order to accept this powerful new mill, with upgrade modifications made in the radiator and fan. Powertrain changes included stronger driveshafts and an improved suspension system. The L78 was available only with four-speed transmission. The car magazines of the time were impressed nearly beyond words, calling the 396 'Vette a "brute."

The 1966 Corvette saw the introduction of the monstrous 427-cubic-inch powerplant. Two versions were available, the L72, rated (conservatively!) at 425 horses, and the tamer L36, advertised at 390. A special power bulge hood came on all 427-equipped 'Vettes.

The L72 produced significantly more performance than the 396 L78, pumping the torque up from the L78's 415 to a stump-pulling 460 foot-pounds. The engine, which completely filled the 'Vette's engine compartment, featured solid lifters and was capable, according to *Car and Driver* magazine, of producing 12-second runs on the dragstrip at over 112 miles per hour. Standard transmission was a four-speed. With somewhat reduced drivability and an extra option cost of $312, the L72 'Vette was just a little too much for some; still, a rather healthy production run of 5,258 L72-powered machines rolled off the line in 1966. The L72 option lasted only one more year before succumbing to even bigger numbers in 1967.

The Corvette first received the tri-carbed 427 engine in 1966.

If you wanted to sport that prestigious 427 emblem on the front fender but keep your 'Vette a little more streetable, then the L36 427 was your ticket. Carrying hydraulic lifters instead of the L72's solid units, the idle of this 390-hp version purred more like a street vehicle's than a race car's. The L36 versions also sold well that first year, with 5,116 produced.

In 1967 came the biggest horsepower numbers ever for the 'Vette. The capable 427 was kicked up a few notches with both 430 and 435-horsepower versions available. The L36 was still in position, immediately followed by the L68 400-horsepower engine. This was a $305 option, and 3,832 were produced.

The 435-hp L71 engine ($437 extra) was something else. With three carbs, solid lifters, and high-compression heads, those in the know indicated that the published horsepower figure was far below its actual value. This powerplant could really flatten you in your seat. The L71, available from 1967 to 1969, was the only Corvette engine ever to use three carburetors. Production for the L71-engined machines was highest in 1967, with 3,754, tailing off to 2,898 in '68 and 2,722 in its final year. A demon on the dragstrip, the L71 cars are highly desirable collectables in the 1990s. During the late 1980s, the 435-hp 'Vettes increased in value at an amazing pace. If you can get a good deal on one of these cars, don't hesitate.

If the L71 wasn't enough as is, it could also be ordered with aluminum cylinder heads for an additional $368. The modified L71 was called the L89 and rated at an identical 435 horses, but once again that figure was far below the

This mighty 435-hp L71 'Vette engine wears a distinctive triangular air cleaner.

actual power to the ground. Very few of this unique model were produced, possibly as few as 16.

The truly awesome L88 Corvette appeared in 1967. This was a limited production model and only 20 were produced that first year. Outwardly, it didn't appear any different from any other 427 'Vette, but once you fired it up, you learned that this was a different beast. It wasn't built for the street, it was built to race. And race it did; it was a real tiger in SCCA (Sports Car Club of America) competition.

The L88 engine featured an unheard-of 12.5 : 1 compression ratio, aluminum heads, four-bolt mains, aluminum pistons, forged rods, and a Holley 850 CFM carb sitting topside. With an extremely high idle speed, it wasn't exactly what you wanted to drive to the grocery store. Dragstrip performance for this machine saw elapsed times close to the 11-second category at about 115 miles per hour. Even though the L88 was never advertised for public consumption, word got around, and a limited number were purchased each year (116 in 1969, its final year; two all-aluminum-engined ZL1 Corvettes were also built in 1969).

The 1967 high-performance engine lineup continued into 1968, along with a brand-new body design for the Corvette. All the same 427 powerplants were available, but this would be the last year for the venerable 327 small-block, which had been introduced with the 1962 model. The top 327 in 1968 was the 350-hp L79 version, a $105 option. The most potent 327, though, was introduced

The L88 427 was a low-production race engine with only 20 built in 1967, its first year. The engine produced 11-second performance on the dragstrip. The L88s were available through 1969.

The L88 was not intended for street use but for racing, as evidenced by this slightly modified 1967 Sting Ray coupe.

earlier in the decade — the fuel-injected L84, which grew from 360 horses in 1963 to 375 in 1965. The L76, last offered in 1965, was the most powerful carbureted 327 with 365 horsepower. No ho-hum performers, these 327 powerplants, and the cars are increasing in value. They will certainly never approach the prices of the 427-powered vehicles, but with their high production numbers, they are going to be around for years to come.

Corvette's big news for 1969 was the introduction of the L46 350-cubic-inch engine, rated at 350 horsepower. This was basically the same old 327 with an increase in stroke and a hydraulic lift camshaft.

The next year saw the debut of the ultimate small-block, the legendary LT1. Its performance add-ons included an aluminum intake manifold, high-compression heads, and an 800 CFM Holley four-barrel carb. The LT1 was rated at 370 horses — very heavy performance for a small-block. It wasn't cheap, either, costing an additional $447 for the option. The LT1's horsepower dropped to 350 in 1971 and a lowly 255 a year later. By 1973, it was gone.

In 1970, the casual observer would have believed that the horsepower race was continuing as a new 454-cubic-inch engine replaced the powerful 427 family. Such was not the case, however, as only one version of the new engine was available, the LS5 with "only 390" horses. It was a time of change for the whole muscle car industry and this downturn in power signaled a trend that continued into the early 1970s.

A special version of the L89 engine was available in limited numbers in 1969. Carrying a 435-horse rating, about 300 of the model were produced.

The 454-powered 'Vette had a formidable opponent, and it was wearing the Chevy Bowtie label. The small-block LT1 produced only 20 fewer horses than the 454, and it was a much better handling machine. For that and other reasons, just 4,473 LS5 454 Corvettes were built in 1970. By 'Vette standards, the 454 hung around for a long time — till 1974, when, for all practical purposes, the Corvette muscle car era ended, with the 350 engine the largest powerplant available.

There was also a mystery LS7 454 powerplant in 1970, but best sources indicate that this engine was never installed in any factory Corvettes. There might have been, however, some dealer-installed LS7s running around loose.

In 1971, a 425-horse version of the 454, the LS6, was available in the 'Vette. Even though the compression ratio had been appreciably reduced to 9:1, this engine, with its increased cubic inches, domed pistons, and 800 CFM Holley was an excellent power producer. The LS6 proved to be a much better street vehicle than the early 427 engines. It would, however, be available for only this model year, only 188 were built. It goes without saying that it's a valuable find today.

There are still those who will argue that the Corvette is not a muscle car, but considering the magnificent big-block powerplants that were available in it, it's hard not to make the association. We're certainly putting the Corvette on our list of muscle cars.

El Camino

The key term in this book is muscle *cars*. So what's a truck doing here? Well, you can argue that the El Camino — and its Ford counterpart, the Ranchero — aren't really trucks at all, but cars with a place to haul cargo. Whether truck or car, performance capabilities of the El Camino closely paralleled the Chevelle lines.

The El Camino was actually based on Chevelle sheet metal, but it never carried the Chevelle nameplate.

The power buildup for the sporty truck started in 1966. Previously, the biggest powerplant available was the venerable 327. But in '66, the 396-cubic-inch rat motor reared its powerful head for some high-speed hauling capabilities. Both the L35 325-hp and L34 360-hp versions were available. Either a four-speed or a Powerglide transmission was available with the 325-hp version, while either a three- or four-speed close-ratio transmission was mandatory for the 360-hp engine.

The following year, the horsepower of the 396 big-blocks changed slightly, with the L35 version again advertised at 325 horses while the L34 version was now rated at 350. Two hot 327s, the L30 and the L79, were no slouches either, with 275 and 325 horsepower ratings, respectively.

Even though the big-block El Caminos were mechanically and functionally equivalent to their Chevelle SS brethren, they did not actually carry the Super Sport nomenclature or nameplates until 1968. For the completely restyled '68 El Camino, the two big-block 396 engines remained available, along with 250-, 275- and 325-horse versions of the 327. There was certainly power aplenty for doing whatever work had to be done—that is, of course, if you were willing to do work with a vehicle as attractive as the El Camino.

The SS396 emblems affixed to the tailgate and front fenders signified that the big mill was sitting under the hood for the 1969 model. The Super Sport was the only model for which the top powerplant could be ordered. Three versions of the 396 engine were available in 1969, with the newest being the brutish 375-horse L78 version. In addition, a 350 engine could be specified with either 250 or 300 horses.

The first year for the powerful 454-cubic-inch powerplant was 1970. Two versions would be available, the Z15, capable of 360 horses, and a howling Z15/LS6 version with an advertised 450-horse rating. When carrying one of these bruiser mills, the utilitarian El Camino looked like this. Anyone want to argue that it's not a muscle car?

Big news for 1970 was that two new 400+-cubic-inch engines were introduced. Actually, though, this was just one new engine, since the LS3 400-cubic-inch powerplant was only a slightly bored-out 396. This engine was rated at 330 horses. The 396 tag stayed with this engine, however, because of the popularity of the number. The Z25 version of the 396 was also still around in a 350-horse version.

The *bigger* news for 1970 was the introduction of two versions of the 454-cubic-inch engine. The so-called Z15 option provided 360 horsepower, while the powerful Z15/LS6 was worth an additional 90 horses. The LS6 carried a special camshaft, mechanical lifters, 11.25:1 compression ratio, and dual exhausts. Either of these low-production 454 El Caminos would be a real find for the muscle car collector.

El Camino performance fell off slightly in 1971, with the top 350 engine dropping off to 270 horses and the top 454 now producing only 425. The bored-out 396 (finally officially called the 400) was rated at 300 horsepower. Like its Chevelle brothers, the performance status of the El Camino was starting on an inevitable downward trend.

In 1972, the single available 454 engine was now only capable of 270 horses (with the Super Sport only), while the 400 topped out at a weak 240 horsepower. The two versions of the 350-cubic-inch engine were now capable of only 175 and 165 net horsepower. The once-powerful engines of the late 1960s were being strangled by low compression ratios and government regulations.

A year later, the single 454 engine was down again, this time to 245 net horses, while the 350 engine carried 175 and 145 ratings. The 454 engine was offered for the last time in 1975, but at only 215 horsepower, it hardly deserved to use the numbers. The 400 bit the dust one year later with a sad rating of 175 net horsepower.

The numbers of El Caminos still around seem very low, with few of them seen at car shows or auctions. But in the 1990s, the big-block versions of these unique machines will become popular. Maybe most of these cars were worked to death and retired, but more of them must be out there. The El Camino would definitely be a good investment for the 1990s.

Monte Carlo Super Sports

Luxury and elegance were two of the big motivations of Chevy engineers when they introduced the brand-new Monte Carlo in 1970. Those goals were certainly achieved, but the Monte Carlo also ended up with one other significant design characteristic in certain models. When some big engines were dropped in under the Monte Carlo's bonnet, the model became a muscle car of sorts, but its performance was far off that of its Chevy brothers.

The Monte Carlo was actually introduced quite late in the muscle car era—actually at the beginning of the end—and then it didn't stay around for very long. But the model was provided immediately with the huge 454-cubic-inch engine, so there was no long buildup in power. The Monte got the biggest there was in the Chevy camp right off the bat.

The Monte Carlo, again because or its luxury image, is somewhat of a sleeper muscle car. But Chevy fans are starting to realize that it's becoming more and more desirable.

The 454-cubic-inch engine was definitely needed to push the Monte Carlo, since the car weighed a hefty 3460 pounds. But the SS454 got the 360-horsepower version of the motor.

Even so, the machine was no match for the real muscle cars of the day, running the quarter-mile in the 16-second range. As was the case with a number of other Chevy products during this period, you could also acquire the 390-hp and the (LS6) 450-hp versions of the 454. Needless to say, today those are desirable machines indeed. In the non-Super Sport models, the L48 350-cubic-inch, 300-hp and 400-cubic-inch, 330-hp powerplants were available.

Along with special suspension equipment, the SS454 package also included the Turbo Hydramatic transmission and power disc brakes. A black-and silver lower trim stripe carried the SS 454 designation just forward of the front door's front crease.

Even with its unique looks and performance capabilities, the Monte Carlo Super Sport did very poorly in the showroom that first year, with only 3,823 being sold.

Even fewer of the SS454s were sold in 1971—only 1919—making Chevy wonder if it had made a big mistake with the introduction of the model. Changes were minimal for the 1971 model year, with two versions of the 454 available: the LS5, worth 365 horses, and the LS6, measured at 425 horsepower. With the standard Monte Carlo, the 350 (245-horse version) and 400-cubic-inch, 300-hp engines could be ordered—a smart move at the time, considering the ever-increasing insurance rates.

Although the Monte Carlo had more of a luxury-car image, there was still power aplenty to push the weighty machine. The model carried both the 400 and 454 power plants. Look closely and you can just make out the SS454 emblem behind the front wheel.

For the 1971 model, GM seemed to be trying to hide the fact that major horsepower was resting under the longest hood in Chevy history. No SS454 identification appeared anywhere on the front of the top-line model to announce its big-block engine, and what emblems were on the car were practically invisible. There was a conflict of images here, and the Monte Carlo suffered because of it.

In 1972, the performance-oriented Monte Carlo was stone dead. In fact, anything to do with performance or a racy appearance was actually mocked in the Monte Carlo national advertising campaign. A greatly derated 454 engine could still be ordered, but it put out only 270 horses. The final year a 454 could be acquired was 1975, but its horsepower had dropped to half its original rating.

Nova Super Sports

A nice, quiet, boxy little car, something to pick up groceries in, something that the English teacher at the local high school might drive — that was the image the Chevy II and its follow-up Nova had during the early 1960s. But during the last half of the decade, monumental changes abounded with the model. Surprisingly, though, the evolution of the Nova into a legitimate muscle car was a secret to many. Muscle just didn't fit the Nova's image.

The Nova move from mush to muscle began in 1966, when a brand-new body style was introduced. It was shorter and more than an inch wider, with flat sides and a whole new rear-end treatment. The '66 Nova SS model featured lower body trim and Super Sport lettering on the rear quarters. Along with additional interior appointments, the SS package cost an additional $159.

There was power aplenty to go with the new Nova look, including the potent L30 275-hp version of the tried-and-true 327 powerplant. The real killer,

Possibly the most desirable of all Novas is the 1966 L79. Tom Migut of Illinois owns this beautiful example.

L79 Nova engines featured a dual-snorkel air cleaner unique to the model.

though, was the single-year L79 version of the 327 mill, which was capable of an impressive 350 horses. The L79's power, combined with the Nova's light weight, made the machine a real street performer. The machine was a hit with the performance-minded, and 5,481 were sold. Today, it's among the most desirable vintage small-block muscle machines.

In 1967, the L30 engine was available again, but this would also be its last year. It's also a very desirable collectible, even though it's a small-block machine.

For 1968, the L48 350-cubic-inch engine with a 295-horsepower rating would be the standard powerplant in the completely restyled Nova SS. The SS350 package featured simulated scoops on the hood, blacked-out grille and real deck panel, and front and rear SS tags. With stiff competition from the other General Motors performers, only 4,670 of the spiffy machines were sold.

To increase that ever-important performance image, Chevy also dropped the awesome L78 375-hp 396 into a limited number of SS Novas. Only 667 were built, along with another 234 produced with the L34 350-horse version of the 396. If you wanted the best, though, there was the L89 396 version, which had the same 375-hp rating as the L78, but carried aluminum heads.

The 396 identification for all 1968 versions of the engine was carried on the front fenders next to the SS marking. The performance of these cars was outstanding in national-level competition. Needless to say, finding one of these rare big-block Novas today would be a monumental accomplishment. There were

The final year for a big-block in the Nova was 1970. There were two versions of the 396 (actually 402-cubic-inches), but their numbers were very limited. Dan and Donna Gorby of Dayton, Ohio, are the proud owners of this one.

also 50 specially built COPO 396 Novas, but very little data is available on them. Don't get your hopes up—these cars are very rare.

The L48 396 engine picked up five horsepower for 1969, a year that brought a minimal number of changes in the outward appearance of the SS. Quietly, though, it was still possible to acquire specially prepared Nova Super Sports that carried both the 375-hp L78 and the 350-hp L34 versions of the 396, as well as a 325-horse version. The L78 generated the most interest, with 5262 sold, while 1947 of the milder L34s were driven home. Apparently most buyers figured that if you were going to lay down the big bucks for a 396 Nova, you might as well get the most potent of the 396 trio.

Then came the ultimate—the Yenko SC 427 Nova. The engines were not factory-installed, but were squeezed into position by the Yenko Chevrolet dealership in Canonsburg, Pennsylvania. They were few in number—30, to be exact. The cars arrived at the dealership carrying L78 396 engines, which were replaced by L72 427-cubic-inch, 425-horsepower mills. With their distinctive Yenko markings, similar to those on the Yenko conversions of the Camaro and Chevelle, these rare machines are probably the most desirable of the Nova supercars. Very few have been found.

Reportedly, a very small number of factory 427 Novas were built. Only about half a dozen of these cars have been located and their values make them—along with the Yenko Novas—the best of the muscle Novas. In the early 1990s, their values might well escalate to six figures.

Moving on to 1970, the standard engine for the Nova SS was a 300-hp version of the new 350 engine. Although the L34 and L78 396 versions weren't advertised in the showroom literature, they could still be had. The 396 engines were now actually 402 cubic inches, but, like other versions of Chevy muscle machines, the models were marketed with the now-familiar 396 numbers. Altogether, 3,765 of the L78 Novas hit the street (or, more likely, the strip) in 1970, while 1,802 customers rolled out L34-equipped machines. If you locate one of these cars, don't tell anybody, just go ahead and buy it.

There was yet another Nova for 1970, although it wasn't listed in any sales brochure. Called the Yenko Deuce, it carried the LT1 Corvette version of the 350 engine, which knocked out 370 willing ponies. Other power-train components included the Turbo 400 transmission controlled by a Hurst shifter and a 12-bolt 4.11 rear end. There's no way not to recognize one of these Novas, as the Deuce featured a body-length stripe which swept over the rear fender with "Yenko Deuce" lettered within. The stripes then swept over the rear deck. The LT1 was announced in big block letters on the hood. The modified Nova model sold only 176 copies.

Bye-bye Nova big-blocks for 1971—it was the beginning of the end for high-powered Novas and this year the trend took a giant step downward. The new Rally Nova model featured a 245-hp version of the 350, while the Super Sport version of the 350 produced only 270 horses on regular gas.

But hang on—rumor has it that during the 1971 model year, some Novas were equipped with 454-cubic-inch 450-horsepower mills. At this time, the 454s were available in the Monte Carlo and Chevelle, so anything is possible. If such cars were built, many Chevy fans are still waiting to see one. And if one is found and verified, it will be worth pure gold.

After 1972, the Nova could no longer be classified as a muscle car. By 1973, for example, the L48 had been strangled to only 175 net horsepower. Even with the power reduction, though, the Nova SS continued to be a good seller. It was a time of scarce and expensive oil, so a gas-guzzling big-block wasn't a favorite mode of transportation.

It is probably that old grocery-getter image that causes many to shake their heads when muscle cars and the Nova are mentioned in the same breath. But the Nova deserves its place in the history of muscular machines. These cars will be heard from in the years to come.

The Fabulous 409s

Four-Oh-Nine: Those three magic numbers were immortalized in a rockin' song by the Beach Boys in the 1960s. Chevy's 409-cubic-inch engine was literally part of the American culture of the early 1960s—and besides that, it could run like crazy. First appearing in 1961, the Biscaynes, Bel Airs, and Impalas that carried the mighty power plant were some of the fastest machines of the time. And the 409 was only the vanguard of a lot more muscle to come from Chevy in the near future.

Despite all the publicity the 409 engine received, amazingly few of the cars were produced—only about 43,000 during its five production years, 1961 through 1965.

The 409 was not a new engine built from scratch for high-performance, but an evolution of the 1950s-vintage 348-cubic-inch truck engine. Although the 348

The Impala—like this '62 convertible—was one of several body designs that carried the 409 powerplant. Biscaynes and Bel Airs also could be ordered with the famous 409.

was a reliable powerplant, the initial 409s in 1961 lacked the same quality. However, the following year, a number of changes were made, including beefing up the block and heads. Then, with the addition of a second four-barrel carb, the horsepower rating of the 409 matched its cubic inches, a notable technical accomplishment.

The powerplant carried solid lifters, an 11:1 compression ratio, and a progressive linkage setup to operate the second carburetor. The early monster motor was capable of 420 foot-pounds of torque. Punching the pedal to the floor in a 409-powered machine buried the driver in the seat as the engine's power and torque just seemed to go on forever.

A single-carb version of the 409 became available in 1962. Certainly no slouch, the version was capable of a none-too-shabby 380 horses.

Those famous 409 grey valve covers announced the powerful figures with 409 Turbo-Fire decals on the top and either 409 or 380 Horsepower on the bottom. A total of 15,019 409-engined vehicles were produced in 1962, compared to only 142 in 1961.

For 1963, the L33 version of the 409 was introduced. This single-carbureted engine (which had no 409 decals) sported a hydraulic camshaft, aluminum pistons, a lower 10:1 compression ratio, and an abundance of chrome engine detailing.

For the real adventure-minded, there was the L80 409. Would you believe 425 horses to light your fire and burn the tread right off the tires? If you were looking for gas mileage, this was definitely not the engine option for you. However, if you had known at the time the value of the powerplant today, it

Evolving from the 348-cubic-inch Chevy truck engine, the twin-carb version of the 409 in 1962 put out a screaming 409 horsepower.

would have been an immediate choice. It's a very desirable powerplant to own these days.

The biggest of the 1963 409s carried twin aluminum carbs, a twin-snorkel air cleaner, and upgraded valves and heads. It was a very expensive option at $484. There was one other 409 version for 1963, the L31, which produced a "mere" 400 horses.

The three 409 options remained unchanged for 1964, but the competition caught up and passed the 409 in performance and cubic inches. The 421 Pontiacs, 426 Hemi-powered MOPAR machines and 427 Fords were now stomping the 409 at the dragstrips.

The 409's final farewell came in 1965, when the 425-hp version was removed from the books. Only 2,828 of the two lower-power versions were built that last year.

One of the more interesting aspects of the 409-powered cars were the so-called plain-Jane Bel Airs and Biscaynes that carried the powerplant. A number of these cars have been located and restored. Just sitting at the stoplight, they gave no indication of what was under the hood with their economy interior, cheap hubcaps, and obvious lack of chrome. But a glance at the 409 tag on the front fender changed everything.

You could also have a little luxury with your 409 in the Impala Super Sport. Everybody knew the Impala was a muscle car; it was more fun to fool 'em with a stripped-down 409 Bel Air or Biscayne.

A high-powered variation of the basic 409 Impala was the so-called Z11. This extremely limited production model carried a 409 power plant that had been bored and stroked to 427 cubic inches. It cost $1237 extra to acquire this 430-horsepower, twin-carbed demon. Only about 57 of these powerplants were built, with some going in Impalas with lightened aluminum front ends. A number of these cars have been located and restored.

The famous old 409 engine set the trend for the big-block muscle cars of the early 1960s. Today, the 409 cars bring the big bucks and that trend is not likely to change. Think it's got anything to do with that famous Beach Boys tune?

OLDSMOBILE DIVISION

A popular advertisement today states that the new Olds is "Not your father's Oldsmobile." The idea behind the slogan, of course, is that the new car isn't stuffy and boring. Nice ad, but if your father happened to own certain Olds models during the late 1960s or early 1970s, the slogan takes on a meaning quite opposite the one intended. The family of 4-4-2s, W machines, and Hurst/Olds models represented high-performance personified and today are still some of the most desirable vintage muscle machines going.

4-4-2 and the W Machines

It all started for Olds quite obscurely in 1964, when the 4-4-2 was offered as a performance option. As was the case through the 1966 model year, the 4-4-2 equipment could be ordered in both the F-85 and Cutlass body styles. Only 2,999 4-4-2s were sold that first year, but things soon took off for Olds.

The 4-4-2 package appeared somewhat sedate when compared to the big-block powerplants available from Ford and Chrysler, but the B09 package was a great start. Power came from the L78 330-cubic-inch, 310-horse powerplant, while other pieces in the package included special suspension components, heavy-duty brakes, and a fully synchronized four-speed transmission. A 4-4-2 so equipped could be had for just $2,784 — certainly a hard-to-believe figure in the 1990s!

Olds quickly realized that it had a winner on its hands and pumped up the horses the following year; 1965 saw the engine cubes move up to 400 and the horsepower to 345. The new power train was designated the W-29 option, and 25,003 so-equipped models were sold that year. Olds definitely was getting the attention of the performance-minded.

The horsepower wars were now on in earnest, and, to compete, Oldsmobile launched a late-1965 charge with the potent L69 tri-carbed motor, introduced during the '66 model year. The available 360 horses pushed the L69-engined models to the front of the musclecar battle.

But there was to be even more for 1966. Enter the first of the mighty W machines, the W-30, an upgrade of the L69 engine system. Well, that's not quite true, since a little-known W-29 designation was used to cover the 1965–1967 4-4-2s. The W-30, though, was the first W that would be carried on the 4-4-2's

The first W-30 powerplant had 400 cubic inches and produced an impressive 350 horses with 440 foot-pounds of torque. Note the unique air cleaner configuration.

sheet metal, and having it there makes the model a very attractive muscle car for the current investor. A '66 W-30 would be a sweet find indeed, since only 54 were built, all of them Cutlass hardtops. There were others, however, since it is known that a number of W-30s were converted by Olds dealers. The L69-equipped machines were much more plentiful, with 2,129 F-85 and Cutlass models being so equipped in 1966, the only year the L69 engine was offered.

The W-30 modification was basically a strengthening of the L69 engine, including the addition of stronger valve springs, a new hotter camshaft, and a cold-air induction system, which supplied air directly to the trio of Rochester carbs. In an official Olds photo of the W-30 engine, the scoops look like two giant vacuum cleaners—and that's pretty much the purpose they served.

The word was out on the W-30 for 1967 and production increased to 502. Olds fans liked the continuing engine refinements, along with the chromed dual-snorkel air cleaner. Weight reduction was accomplished in an eye-striking manner with red fiberglass inner fenders. It was hard to believe that they were stock, but they were. The battery was moved to the trunk and a new ignition system kept things perking under the hood.

A total of 1,911 of the W-30s were sold in 1968, the second-best year for the option (behind 1970). It was also the best year for the 4-4-2, with 36,641 sold. The $263 W-30 option in its third year would continue to feature the induction

This magnificent 1968 4-4-2 convertible carries the 400-cubic-inch powerplant. It's owned by the Saudys family of Columbus, Ohio.

The so-called Ram Rod 350 was the lead-in engine to the W-31 motor. In many ways, it was a miniature version of the W-30.

This Ram Rod Cutlass is owned by Dean Pacard of Springfield, Ohio.

scoops along with additional refinements to the 400-cubic-inch engine. The W-30 power train had matured to stand with the big boys. Specially modified W-30s demonstrated quarter-mile performance of 12 seconds at over 110 miles per hour.

The next W number was 31, and the model was an interesting experiment. The W-31 was built on the 350 engine instead of the 400, but it was a far cry from the standard 350. It materialized in 1968 as the so-called W-31 Ram Rod. In many ways, the W-31 was a miniature version of the W-30 engine, with its below-bumper scoops, dual-snorkel air cleaner and dual exhausts. The W-31 was a rocket, capable of 13-second quarters. The single-year $263 option was easily identified by a decal on the front fenders showing an end view of two pistons

In case you've never seen one, here's a closeup of the Ram Rod front fender decal.

The W-31 powerplant appeared in 1968 and was based on the 350 powerplant. The W-31 was available in either the F-85 or the Cutlass, like this 1970 model.

and rods hooked to a crank and the lettering Ram Rod 350. A few of the Ram Rods are still around, but not many, since only 742 were ever built.

A number of "plain" W-31s were also built. The W-31 option was available on both the F-85 and Cutlass models and was identified by a W-31 on the front fenders. The W-31s were built through the 1970 model year.

The W-32 was the third and last of the W cars. With only 297 produced in 1969, the only year of its production, the W-32 is by far the rarest of the W cars. Simply put, the W-32 was a more drivable and streetable version of the W-30. It carried the same 400-cube powerplant as the W-30, but its engine purred instead of emitting the bumpy rumble of the W-30. The W-32 buyer got all the looks of the W-30, and if you own one today, you've got one very desirable muscle machine.

For 1970, Olds introduced a big increase in cubic inches—to 455—for both the 4-4-2 and the W-30. The 4-4-2 got a 455-cubic-inch engine with a 10.5 : 1 compression ratio, hydraulic lifters, and a Rochester four-barrel carburetor; horsepower was advertised at 365, five less than the W-30 version. The main difference in the two powerplants was the W-30's aluminum intake manifold. At the peak of the horsepower era the 455 machines made a big hit, with 3100 of the big block W-30s built.

The tumble for the W-30 began in 1971 with the dramatic reduction of compression ratios; 70 horsepower were lost from the powerful engine. The W-30 cars showed a corresponding popularity drop, with only 920 constructed along with only 7589 4-4-2s, down from 19,330 the year before. No W-31s were built.

The last year for the W-30 was 1972, but the car didn't really deserve the magic numbers. Horsepower had dropped off to 300 and the interest in the model was also waning, with the year's production run totalling 772. The 4-4-2 was also terminated as a model and put back on the option shelf.

The Rallye 350 was an interesting one-year Olds muscle car in 1970. The Sebring Yellow (only color) sporty machine carried a 310-horse version of the 350 engine.

Rallye 350

During 1970, Olds produced another interesting one-year performance car, the Rallye 350. This machine was painted in bright Sebring Yellow with stylish orange and black striping—it certainly got your attention. The W45 Rallye package provided an abundance of extra equipment, including a twin-scooped fiberglass hood, sport mirrors, custom steering wheel, Rally suspension, and rear spoiler. Also standard with the Rallye was the Endura urethane bumper. The Rallye 350's engine was not quite up to the W-31 350, putting out 15 fewer horses at 310.

Hurst/Olds

But there was one other Olds muscle car for the period, the Hurst/Olds 4-4-2s. Several Hurst/Olds served as Indy pace cars during the period. The Hurst machines used the 455 engine modified to produce 390 horses.

The first 1968 Hurst/Olds showed a production run of only 515. In 1969—again with the 455-hp powerplant—production increased to 914. The modifications would continue to appear through the 1970s and beyond.

"Not your father's Oldsmobile"—you'd better believe it! These vintage Oldsmobiles were real big-block roaring machines.

The Hurst/Olds modifications introduced the 455 powerplant in 1968. This photo shows the 1969 H/O engine configuration.

PONTIAC DIVISION

Three-letter names were popular for '60s muscle cars, and most of them were meaningless. But the meaning of "GTO" is easy to determine. It stands for "Grand Turismo Omologato," a European term meaning *homologated* (standardized and approved) for Grand Touring racing. The GTO label was originally applied to a Ferrari sports racer, and the sexy-sounding name was shamelessly appropriated by Pontiac for its premier muscle line.

The GTO letters are extremely significant in the story of American muscle. Simply put, the GTO was the first '60s muscle car to be merchandised as a high-performance machine for the masses. Granted, there were earlier muscle cars, but they didn't fulfill this particular criteria.

GTO

Pontiac's GTO was officially introduced in late 1963 and was immediately accepted by the public. The look and performance were exactly right for the time. The car's background is interesting in that this buildup of engine performance conflicted with Pontiac's official policy of backing off from its factory drag-racing activities earlier in the year. Also during this period, GM was banning power plants greater than 330-cubic-inches in mid-sized cars. This would obviously be a problem if there was to be a big-block GTO. The solution was a bit on the sneaky side, to say the least. What Pontiac did was make the big-engined GTO an option of the Tempest line.

With the GTO option, the buyer got a machine that could pulverize the Saturday night opposition in any stoplight challenge. Two quick-revving 389-cubic-inch powerplants were available during the first three years of the option. Both versions carried special HO heads, high-performance valve springs, and a high-lift cam. The 335-horsepower version came equipped with a Carter four-barrel carb, while the heads were borrowed from the 421-cubic inch Super Duty powerplants developed during Pontiac's earlier drag-racing exploits.

But what really caught the attention of the performance-minded was the so-called "Tri-Power" option. This produced an additional 13 horsepower by way of an impressive row of three Rochester two-barrel carbs. For normal driving duties, the motor hummed along on the center carb only. Punch the pedal and the outer two came to life—then stand back and get the women and children off the streets!

The Tri-Power versions of the 1964 through 1966 GTOs are the most desirable of the breed, commanding considerably higher prices than the single four-barrel carb versions. The fact that 34,450 GTOs were sold the first year

The 389 Tri-Power engine was one of the great features of the 1964-through-1966 GTOs. The Tri-Power (1965 version shown here) had 348 horses in 1964 and 360 in '65 and '66.

means that quite a few must still be around. Like many mid-1960s muscle cars, many of these early GTOs were "daily drivers" until the late 1970s, when they became recognized as classics. Suddenly the vintage GTOs started getting new attention and care from their owners.

During the final two years of the Tri-Power option, the horsepower rating increased from its initial 348 to 360. The single four-barrel version also picked up 10 horsepower (to 335) in 1965 and 1966.

The 1964 GTO looked a lot like the Tempest LeMans because that's exactly what it was. GTO identifiers included the GTO nameplates on the left side of the split grille, the rear flanks, and the right side of the rear deck, along with the 6.5-liter engine designation on the front quarters.

Through the three 389-cubic-inch engine years, power train options included both automatic and three- and four-speed transmissions, along with a number of rear axle ratios.

When the '65 "Goat" (a name affectionately given the GTO) appeared, the model had gained its own identity and the event was celebrated with a complete facelift. Voted the most popular GTO ever, the 1965 version was no longer a touched-up LeMans, but now spoke in bold terms that it was a muscle machine on the move.

Major changes in the model included the stacked headlights and a redesigned hood. Twin exhaust pipes emerged from behind the rear wheels. The buying public loved it, and Pontiac sold 75,352 copies, far above what its management had projected.

With almost a hundred thousand (96,946 to be exact) completely restyled GTOs sold in 1966, changes were afoot in this third year. The '66 engine options remained the same, but this would be the final year for the 389 powerplant.

This gorgeous 1966 GTO carries a 389 four-barrel power plant. The Goat is owned by John Holder of Little Rock, Arkansas.

General Motors dictated that there would be no more three-carb set-ups, even though the success of the arrangement had been phenomenal.

From 1966 to 1969, some special GTOs were modified by the Royal Pontiac dealership in Detroit. Coined the Royal Bobcat GTOs, the machines carried unique striping and engine upgrading. Much like the Yenko modifications on Chevy muscle cars, these cars will continue to generate considerable collector interest.

The appearance of the 1967 Goat was little changed from '66, but under the hood it was all-new. The new cubic-inch number was up 11 cubes over the previous 389, and two versions of the new 400 powerplant were available. The standard engine came with a four-barrel carb with the horsepower rated at the same 335 figure as the four-barrel version of the 389 engine. The performance-minded could get an additional 25 horses from a 400 HO (high output) powerplant. There was also a 400-cubic-inch Ram Air I version (same 360 horsepower rating), which sold 751 copies.

A brand-new body greeted GTO fans in 1968. Major changes included the return to horizontal headlights, decal GTO emblems on the rear quarters, the optional Enduro bumper, and functional hood air scoops for the Ram Air engine option. The 400 Ram Air was again rated at 360 horses, 10 more than the upgraded-for-1968 standard 400 engine. The Ram Air powerplant also received a midyear update and was given the new name Ram Air II.

For GTO's sixth year, body styling stayed about the same, but changes again abounded under the hood. Even so, the 1969 totals were only 72,287 units sold. The downward trend for the GTO had begun, with only half that number being sold the following year.

Also introduced during 1969 was the special model called the Judge, a GTO offshoot, which is covered in the following section.

For 1970, the 400-cubic-inch powerplant remained standard, but the Ram Air III (366 horsepower) and the Ram Air IV (370 horsepower) were the

The sleek, all-new '68 GTO was *Motor Trend's* Car of the Year.

available high-performance engine options. These powerplants were accompanied by either "Ram Air" or "Ram Air IV" decals on the hood.

The writing was on the wall for the demise of the big-cube powerplants as the GTO entered the 1970s. However, the obvious trouble-ahead indications didn't stave off the introduction of the monster 455-cubic-inch powerplant, rated at 360 horses, in 1970.

The predicted power slide began for the GTO in 1971. The drop in compression ratio (from the tens to the eights) was directly measured in proportional horsepower drops. For example, the 455 engine showed a considerable decrease to 325 horsepower. A low-compression version of the 455 HO engine was listed at 335 horsepower. There was certainly no questioning whether a GTO carried the 455 powerplant, since it was announced loudly in bold letters atop the air cleaner.

In 1972, the GTO suffered a major slap in the face. It no longer was its own series, but reverted to its roots as a derivative of the LeMans. The end was near for the GTO that year, with only 5,807 buyers opting for the package. The horsepower spiral continued downward, with the HO engine now showing only a 300 rating.

For the final two years of the GTO, the once-proud performer could hardly be called a muscle car anymore. It stayed a forgotten LeMans option in 1973 and then moved to the Ventura series (Pontiac's version of the Chevy Nova) the following year. The GTO didn't even look like a GTO anymore; it was just the

The 1971 GTO still had mean looks, but its performance was beginning to fade.

By 1973, GTO was reduced to an option on the LeMans.

famous letters pasted onto a standard passenger car. The biggest horsepower available in 1973 was 250 hp from the once-proud 455, with only 230 horses coming from the 400 motor. The final insult came in 1974 — the GTO's last year of production — when a four-barrel 350-cubic-inch engine could only wheeze out a pathetic 200 horsepower.

From an enthusiastic high-performance start to a sad ending a decade later — that was the story of one of the great muscle cars. While certain other muscle cars of the period were dropped at the peak of their performance, the GTO was allowed to dangle helplessly in the wind as its power and looks were slowly drained from its body.

The Judge

Okay, so the Judge is a GTO. But the low production numbers and unique performance options of the model make it worthy of a section of its own. The flashy Judge has proved to be a muscle car that is escalating rapidly in value and should be a real comer in the 1990s.

When the Judge was first introduced in 1969, it was meant as just a one-year gimmick to boost GTO sales, which were starting to level off at the time. But the Judge would last through the 1971 model year, even though the slicked-up GTO didn't do that well initially with only 6833 copies sold in 1969. The sales dwindled down to 3797 in 1970. Only 108 of the '69 Judges and 168 of the '70 models were convertibles, making those very desirable collectibles. Any 1971 model, since there were only 374 produced, is also highly desirable.

As the GTO started to pick up weight and accessories during the late 1960s, Pontiac began to consider building a modified version to attract the young and performance-minded. The GTO had moved away from its initial performance image of the mid-1960s, and there were those who felt that the muscle car movement would last for many more years, making the Judge production program worthwhile.

Initial Judge plans involved completely stripping down a lightweight Tempest body, installing a 350 HO powerplant, and then putting it up against the hot-selling Plymouth Road Runner competition. This concept, though, eventually evolved into a $332 performance option for the GTO. It was also decided that the 400-cubic-inch, 366-horse Ram Air III would become the Judge's standard powerplant, but there was also an impressive 400-cubic-inch, 370-hp Ram Air IV engine. Although not considered to be a dragstrip challenge to the Hemi-powered cars, the Judge did have its bright times on the strips.

The Judge was officially released on December 19, 1968, and the model definitely stood out from its GTO brothers. The Judge name was announced on each front fender, on the right side of the 60-inch-wide rear spoiler, and on the dash. The GTO nameplate was still carried forward and aft on the body. The initial Judge also featured a distinctive stripe that swept along the top of the front fenders, across the doors, and finished with a flaired kick-up.

In order to really attract attention, the first 2,000 '69 Judges were painted Carousel Red, an eye-popping orange-red, but later it was possible to acquire the car in any standard GTO color.

Lettering on the hood announced the Ram Air III 400 power plant, while Ram Air IV told that the 400-cubic-inch, 370-hp engine was sitting under the hood. It is also rumored that there were a few dealer-installed 428-powered Judges carrying Ram Air IV heads. These initial Judges stickered in the $3500 range—amazing but true!

In 1970, the Judge took on a more distinctive look with twin eyebrow stripes front and rear. Judge decals appeared on the front fenders and on the right side of the rear deck. Again, the Ram Air III was the standard engine and the Ram Air IV was the performance powerplant to really smoke up the bleach box at the local dragstrip.

Wayne Robinson of Columbus, Ohio, loves his 400-cubic-inch-powered Judge. Note the special trim carried by the spruced-up GTO.

The Judge entered its third and final year basically unchanged from 1970. The same teardrop striping remained, and the fact that the vehicle was carrying the LS5 455 HO 335-horse powerplant was announced on each edge of the rear spoiler.

Standard equipment for the last of the Judges included the heavy-duty three-speed transmission controlled by a floor-mounted shifter, Rally II wheels, and various Judge decals. The last Judge was Pontiac's last attempt to prop up the ever-decreasing sales of the GTO. It didn't work, and the Judge was terminated in February 1971.

The rarest of the 1971 models were some 15 Judges produced in Cameo White with black striping and rear wing. The cars were built under an Option RP0604, making them highly desirable.

In terms of collectibility, the Judge rates slightly higher than the standard GTO because of its low production and flashy graphics. Currently bringing in $20,000 and more at the start of the 1990s, the Judge will continue to increase in value.

Grand Prix

Let's generate a little controversy in the Pontiac muscle car arena with the monstrous Grand Prix. The almost two-ton Goliath, first introduced in 1962, certainly didn't have the expected lightweight body of most muscle cars, but its styling through the years and its major-league power have classified it as legitimate muscle in many people's minds.

The SJ Option first became available on the Grand Prix in 1969. Included for the first time was the 455-cubic-inch powerplant capable of 370 horses.

The Grand Prix's trim styling was always its strong point. It featured rocker panel moldings and an anodized grille insert in the initial model. Through 1966, the GP was powered by the four-barrel 389 powerplant. In 1967, it acquired a 350-horse, 400-cubic-inch engine.

In 1969, the Grand Prix line added the SJ option, which was probably the most popular of the breed. The SJ cost an additional $244 and included a number of appearance items. But most importantly, the 455-cubic-inch powerplant with 370 horses was also on board. In 1971, there was also a special Hurst SSJ Grand Prix. Only 200 were built, and they had to be special-ordered. These are very rare and very desirable collector's items.

In the early 1970s, the big-engined Grand Prix went the way of most muscle cars, with compression ratios falling to 8:1 and horsepower figures dropping out the bottom.

T-37 and GT-37

No, these are not designations for Air Force jet trainers, but low-cost muscle cars based on the Tempest. First introduced in 1970, the T-37 was the hardtop version while the GT-37 identified either a hardtop or a post coupe. The cars were advertised as meeting the driving needs of the most discriminating customer. In some ways, the 37s might be thought of as the embodiment of the original Judge concept of a lightweight, low-cost Road Runner fighter.

The T-37 had somewhat of a montage of looks, including a lot of GTO and even a bit of similarity to the Firebird in the grille design. Figures do not exist for the GT-37, but 20,883 T-37s were produced that first year.

It took $2683 to purchase a T-37, but for a few more bucks, two optional powerplants were available. A standard 350-cubic-inch engine was capable of 255 horses, but for those interested in really putting down the opposition, there were the 400-cubic-inch, 330-hp and 455-cubic-inch, 360-hp big-blocks on tap.

The GT-37 was introduced as a low-budget muscle car. The little-known model carried all the available V-8 engines of the time including the 350-, 400-, and 455-cube powerplants. This 1971 GT-37 is owned by Rick Grimes of Xenia, Ohio.

A year later, these unique models were listed under the LeMans label and marketed by Pontiac to attract the performance-minded. A 455 HO powerplant was again the top gun for 1971, producing five more horsepower than the 455 of the previous year. An extra $358 put the big motor under your hood.

The final year for the model was 1971. To many, the existence of these cars is practically unknown, but their very rareness should make them an excellent muscle investment in years to come. Make no mistake about it, there aren't that many T-37s and GT-37s out there.

The Full-Size 421s

If you ever see a Pontiac with the numbers 421 on the front flank, check it out very carefully, because that powerplant made any Pontiac a muscle machine.

There were a number of versions of the famous 421, including a triple-carbed 370-horsepower version that was introduced in 1963. Later versions of the 421, in 1964, had horsepower ratings of 356 and 376.

Earlier, an even more powerful 421 carried a pair of Carter four-barrel carbs. It was called the 421 Super Duty and pumped out an impressive 405 horses. These mighty mills were extremely few in number and could be found in several versions of the Catalina and Grand Prix.

Mike Garblik is justifiably proud of his 421-powered '66 2 + 2 machine. The advertised horsepower of this machine was quoted at 376 and Garblik can tell you that it's still got it!

Firebird and Trans Am

Pontiac's motivation for building the Firebird in the first place was quite simple. It was the Mustang, the unbelievably successful Ford pony car that turned the American automotive business on its ear in 1964. General Motors was taken completely by surprise, and quickly scrambled to come out with competing models of its own. Chevrolet's Camaro was first, to be followed shortly thereafter with the Firebird.

The first Firebird was constructed in January 1967 and released a month later. The 'Bird was available in either a two-door hardtop or convertible, and

The hot number for the initial 1967 Firebird was the Firebird HO, which carried a hopped-up 326-cubic-inch engine with 285 horsepower.

more than 82,000 were produced that first year. Due to their late release, the first Firebirds were designated as 1967½ models.

A number of power train options were available, with an immediate emphasis on performance. The Firebird 326 models featured what was basically the Tempest 326-cubic-inch engine capable of 250 horsepower. Add four-barrel carburetion, dual exhausts, and 10.5:1 compression ratio, and an additional 35 horses became available. Named the 326 HO (high output), this Firebird sported a body-length side stripe with the HO logo embedded in it.

The big guy, though, for the first year was the Firebird 400, using a slightly derated version of the GTO powerplant. In the Firebird, the power rating was 325 horsepower. There were actually two 400 engines with that rating, the standard 400 and the Ram Air 400. Few of the latter were sold because of its extra $600 cost. Considering that the Firebird weighed just a little over 3000 pounds, that 325-hp engine made this one potent combination.

Also available on this 1967½ Firebird was the 325-horsepower, 400-cubic-inch powerplant, a slightly derated version of the GTO engine.

Several body modifications complemented the Firebird 400, including a flashy dual-scoop hood. With the standard 400 powerplant, these scoops were merely nonfunctional add-ons, but with the Ram Air variant, the scoops came to life.

For 1968, the Firebird powerplant family gained additional cubic inches and power. Pontiac added 24 cubic inches to the 326 engine to create the 350 HO, with an impressive 320 horses. Cost of the 350 HO option was $181, which included a column-mounted three-speed transmission, heavy-duty battery, and dual exhausts. The two-barrel version of the standard 350 engine was worth 265 horses.

The Firebird 400 could really light your fire with 330 horses under the hood. Considerable chrome detailing really set the model off, but the buyer had to pay up to $435 for the extra performance. The Ram Air option was also still available, rated at 335 horses, while the 400 HO carried the same rating. Although the exact production breakout by engine type isn't available for 1968, suffice it to say that it was a very good year for the Firebird, with 107,112 sold, of which more than 88,000 were V-8 equipped models.

Considerable appearance updating highlighted the '69 'Birds, and new power under the hood kept up with the appearance. The L30 Firebird 350 and L76 350 HO engines remained basically unchanged with 265 and 325 horsepower, respectively. The W66 400 engine stayed at the 330-hp figure, as did the L74 Ram Air 400.

But one new addition to the Firebird's powerplant parade for 1969 was the L67 Ram Air IV package. The option again featured the same 400-cubic-inch mill, but 345 horses were produced with the addition of a refined valve train and camshaft. The Ram Air IV Firebird was a screamer and today is a great investment—if you can find one.

The restyled 1969 Firebird featured dual headlights, updated dash, and a new hood design.

The big news for 1969, though, was the introduction of the Trans Am option. That's exactly how the first Trans Am was designated—Option Code WS-4 on the Firebird. It was a Firebird, true, but it hardly looked like one. The TA could be ordered with the same L74 power plant used in the Ram Air 400 package, although the L67 engine was standard.

The Trans Am package was expensive—$725 over the base Firebird price—but well worth it. Available only in white with blue body-length stripes, the first Trans Am was built to perform with a heavy-duty suspension system, a one-inch front stabilizer bar, front disc brakes, and a rear deck-mounted wing.

Getting back to the basic Firebird, the 1970 model year (actually, 1970½, since the second-generation Firebird and Camaro didn't appear until February 1970) saw the introduction of a new version, the Firebird Formula 400, which featured distinctive hood-length scoops. Power came from a downgraded 400-cubic-inch engine, which produced only 265 horses. The L74 Ram Air IV engine could be ordered with the Formula, though, for $169 extra. The standard transmission for the 1970 Formula was a Hurst floor-shifted three-speed. A total of 7708 Formulas were built during its first year.

Fewer than half that number of Trans Ams—3196—were constructed during its second model year. The TA, though, looked like it was ready to do road battle with the Y-96 handling package (which featured both front and rear sway bars), variable-ratio steering, a shaker hood scoop, racing mirrors, bucket seats, and front power disc brakes.

Pontiac's 455-cubic-inch engine made its initial appearance in the Formula and Trans Am for 1971. With the Formula, both the 400 and 455 HO engines

The first Trans Am was introduced in 1969 and the first few built carried both the Firebird and Trans Am names on the front fenders. The L67 was the standard engine with the model, although the car could be ordered with the 345 horse L74 motor.

The Firebird was completely restyled for 1970½. The 1971 Trans Am shown here added high-back bucket seats.

were available, with the resulting models identified as Formula 400 or Formula 455, respectively. A total of 7802 Formulas were produced, including those powered by the 350 powerplant (which had been downgraded to a two-barrel carb and 255 horses—hardly musclecar ingredients).

The 400-cubic-inch engine was no longer available in the Trans Am for 1971, just the LS5 455 HO. With only 2116 TAs sold that year, this is indeed a rare collectible today.

Firebird Formula and Trans Am equipment and options remained basically unchanged for 1972, even though high-performance was already in decline with other General Motors products. Production, though, was down for both models, with only 5250 Formulas and 1286 Trans Ams built. Power was on the way down, with the top 350 rated at only 175 horses, two versions of the 400 rated at 250 and 175 horses, and even the 455 HO derated to only 300.

The big news for 1973 was the LS2 455 Super Duty, which came on board with awesome performance capabilities. It was the final gasp of the musclecar era, as other models' power ratings had plummeted. Available in both the Firebird Formula and Trans Am, the SD-455 powerplants were equipped with four-bolt mains, forged pistons and rods, a Quadrajet carb, and special high-flow cylinder heads. The LS2's horsepower rating was 290, but step on the accelerator and you knew that was an understatement. The National Hot Rod Association (NHRA) factored the LS2 at 375 horsepower for competition. That figure was

The LS5 455 HO powerplant was the standard engine for the Trans Am in 1971. The 400-cube engine was no longer available. The giant powerplant was also available with the Firebird Formula that model year.

This 1973 Trans Am carries the standard 455 engine. Note the huge bird decal that completely covers the hood, a trademark of the Trans Am.

The 1974 Firebird and Trans Am got a new nose to meet new federal bumper standards.

probably pretty close to the truth. Both the decreasingly potent 350 and 400 powerplants were also still available.

Only 252 SD-455s were produced in 1973, including both Formula and Trans Am body styles. The Super Dutys are extremely rare and will command a healthy price during the 1990s.

The SD-455 was still around in 1974, the last shining muscle car of the decade. Its horsepower was still rated at 290, far above its fading brothers and the most powerful engine that could be purchased that year. Also available was the L75 400-cube engine, providing 250 net horsepower.

In 1975 it was pretty well over, muscle-wise, for the Firebird and Trans Am. Engine compression ratios had slipped to 7.6:1 and the top 455 (the SD was gone) could only muster 200 net horses.

The Firebird and Trans Am have never commanded the popularity of their General Motors pony car competition, the Camaro. But that should all change in the 1990s, as collectors start to recognize the Pontiac pony cars for their outstanding styling and high performance.

CHAPTER III

Ford Muscle Cars

THE FORD MOTOR COMPANY WAS INVOLVED IN MUSCLE FROM THE beginning. The company was well into high-performance in the late 1950s with the 352-cubic-inch engine; in 1960, Ford even had a 430-cubic-inch powerplant available.

Four versions of the potent 390-cube engine, with the top of the line producing 401 horses, were available in 1961. A year later, a midyear introduction 406-cubic-inch engine plant produced horsepower ratings of 405 and 385.

Later in that muscular decade, Ford's cubic inch and horsepower numbers continued to climb. Different versions of the awesome 427 mill provided well over 400 ponies, while the one-cube-larger 428 was in the mid-300-horse range.

Then there was the 429-cubic-inch engine and its Cobra Jet and Super Cobra Jet variations, with horsepower ratings in the 375 range. Today—as then—these 427- and 429-powered machines are considered the most coveted by Ford muscle fanatics.

Boss was another highly-regarded Ford nameplate of the period, with three high-performance powerplants evolving—the Boss 302, 351, and 429—all wrapped in attractive Mustang sheet metal.

Ford's mighty powerplants were available in a number of different body styles, and many of the Ford supercars also had suspension and handling capabilities to match their muscle. Not only did they look like race cars, they ran like them. Ford also showed little modesty in naming its beasts. You just knew that a car with a name like Cobra Jet, Mach 1, Cyclone, Boss, or Eliminator had to have a ton of performance.

After a slow start in the collector market, the following of Ford muscle cars is starting to increase in the 1990s. Bargains are still out there, but that won't be the case much longer.

FORD MOTOR COMPANY
Mustang

When Ford's Mustang was first introduced in 1964, big muscle under the hood wasn't its main selling point. It was the magnificent styling that caught America's attention and made the Mustang one of the most successful first-year cars ever with more than 100,000 sold.

Muscle would come later in a big way for the Mustang, with a number of impressive big-blocks and special performance models known as Cobra Jet, Mach 1, and Boss. But the first of the Mustang muscle cars—and indeed they were small-block muscle cars—were those powered by the Hi-Po K version of Ford's standard 289-cubic-inch engine.

No big-blocks for the early Mustang—there just wasn't room in those early engine compartments. But the Hi-Po 289 would light your fire in the 2500-pound machines. A fender tag stating 289 High Performance was the only sheet metal identifier of this engine. The K engine was available through the 1967 model year, when the big-block engines made their debut.

Although small in size, the 289 K was capable of a very impressive 271 horsepower. Originally available only with a four-speed transmission, later versions (in 1966 and 1967) would be available with the C4 automatic transmission.

The 289 Hi-Po powerplant was available from 1965 through 1967. It had two power ratings, 271 and 306 horsepower.

The Hi-Po K featured a 10.5:1 compression ratio, a mechanical camshaft, a four-barrel 480 CFM carburetor, solid valve lifters, five main bearings and a four-inch stroke. A number of special handling and suspension items came with this powerplant, making the Hi-Po one of the top performers of its day.

A Hi-Po K under the hood of any early Mustang makes it a highly collectible model, and the variant will find increasing popularity during the 1990s. Back then, though, the K cars' sales figures dropped off badly during its final year, with only 472 sold in 1967.

For its fourth year, the Mustang got a complete restyling. Although it still looked a lot like the original, the whole car was bigger to accommodate the new Code Z 390-cubic-inch powerplant. This potent engine was rated at a street-scorching 315 horses at 4600 rpm. It was available through the 1969 model year and was known as the GT 390 during those years. Designated as Code S engines for 1968 and 1969, the published horsepower for those years was 325 and 320, respectively. Any Mustang model could be ordered with the 390 powerplant (the fastback was a popular body selection). It was an excellent dragstrip performer against the ample GM and Chrysler competition of the time. But the 390 was merely a forerunner of the truly awesome big-block Mustangs that would evolve during the late 1960s.

Mustang Cobra Jet and Mach 1

The next big number for the Mustang would be 428, but before beginning the story of that engine, let's note that there could have been a powerplant with one less cubic inch. However, due to numerous problems with the 427 engine, that powerplant never made it into the 1968 Mustang.

The 428 Cobra Jet engine, which had been used in the full-sized Galaxie since 1966, would be available in the Mustang from mid-1968 through 1970. We're talking real muscle here, with a published horsepower rating of 335, a figure that most considered understated. With the Ram Air system, the engine was denoted Code R, while without Ram Air, the designation was Code Q.

The 428 CJ carried a 10.7:1 compression ratio, a Holley 735 CFM four-barrel carb, and five main bearings. The 428, which had 440 foot-pounds of torque, was also used in a number of other Ford muscle cars, including Cobra Jet Fairlanes and Mercury Cyclones.

During its early production run, many of the 428s were installed in Mustang GT models and later in the Mach 1s. The GTs used the Ram Air option and carried distinctive twin stripes down the center of the hood with 428 lettering. Mustang performance with the Cobra Jet powerplant in place was capable of mid-13-second quarter-mile runs in stock trim, making it considerably faster than its MOPAR and GM competition in the form of Camaro and Chevelle SS396s, GTOs, and even Hemi cars.

An even more potent package with the Cobra Jet engine could be acquired in 1969 in the performance-enhancing Drag Pack. Included in this package were a performance crankshaft, an engine oil cooler, a vibration damper, special connecting rods, and either 3.91 or 4.30 rear end gearing. With the Drag Pack,

Bob Stewart of Huber Heights, Ohio, owns this beautiful 1968 428 Cobra Jet-powered Mustang GT.

the engine was designated the Super Cobra Jet and was capable of 360 horses. Put slicks on this baby and you were talking an easy 12-second car.

Moving up one additional cubic inch, another high-performance engine came into view for the Mustang. The 429 Cobra Jet (available in 1970) and the

The 1968 Cobra Jet Ram Air powerplant boasts 335 horses, certainly an under-rated figure.

This 1969 Mach I carries the 428 Cobra Jet engine.

Super Cobra Jet (1971) were originally planned for even more growth in the future, but that never happened. The 429s were available in all Mustang models in 1971, making these rather interesting muscle machines. For all practical purposes, the sizzling powerplant was around for just one year in the Mustang before emissions requirements put it to bed for good. A very good candidate for muscle car investment in the 1990s, the 429 Cobra Jet was rated at 370 horses while the SCJ kicked out an additional five.

When carrying the Drag Pack option, the horsepower rating of the '69 428CJ was 360.

The 429 Super Cobra Jet powerplant was available in 1971 in several Mustang versions.

The 1971 429SCJ was rated at 370 horsepower.

Boss Mustangs

Performance image machines—that's what you have to call the Boss family of Mustangs. They were racy-looking and had the engines under the hood to back up those looks. The design of the Boss models came under the skilled direction of former General Motors designer Semon Knudsen, whose lone goal was to gain on the opposition.

The 1970 Boss 302 looked like it could go straight from showroom to racetrack.

The Boss 302 engine used a specially selected block that was equipped with screw-in freeze plugs. The engine incorporated heads that were similar to those of the 351-cubic-inch Cleveland engine. The match provided a significant power boost due to more efficient combustion chambers, large valves, and improved breathing capabilities. Horsepower was rated at a healthy 290 at 5800 rpm, with the torque sitting at the same figure. The Boss 302 weighed in at 3227 pounds and was only produced for two years, 1969 and 1970. Production figures for the initial year totalled 1628, with 6318 built in the second and final year.

Racing was the original motivation behind the development of the Boss 302. Chevy's Camaro team under the rule of Roger Penske had been tearing up the SCCA Trans Am racing series and Ford didn't like it. The Boss 302 was the machine Ford used to challenge the GM domination. In 1970, the Mustang put the Camaros in the dust. (By that time, however, Penske had given up his Chevrolets to sign a deal with American Motors.)

With Parnelli Jones at the helm, the team won the Trans Am championship with Jones taking five checkered flags himself. The other team driver, George Folmer, also won one race, giving the Bud Moore Ford team more than half the total 1970 series victories. The team had also run in 1969, but some serious crashes had eliminated them from title contention after winning four races. Ford's involvement in motorsports ended in late 1970, along with the Boss 302—just when the team had reached its peak.

The Boss 302 looked like it could go racing right off the showroom floor and was the only Mustang that carried the Boss 302 powerplant. It was the striping that really set this machine off, with a wide center stripe and two small outer stripes cascading down the hood. Another stripe swept along the body sides from the rear to just forward of the door's front edge, where it changed direction and jumped vertically up the front fender, terminating in 302 lettering. With front and rear spoilers, blacked-out grille and rear window louvers, this was one brutish-looking machine. Even though the Boss 302 carries—by '60s muscle car standards—a somewhat small powerplant, its limited production and racing heritage virtually guarantee sizable price escalations in the 1990s.

The Shaker hood scoop was optional for '70 Boss 302.

Next on the Boss number scale comes the Boss 351, probably the least-known member of the family. The Boss 351 engine would probably have been the powerplant for the Trans Am Mustangs of the early 1970s, but when Ford dropped out of racing, that plan fell by the wayside.

The 351 Mustang was only around for the 1971 model year, but it represented a stout machine for drag racing. The R-Code powerplant was capable of 330 horses and 370 foot-pounds of torque. It carried a Motorcraft 750 CFM carburetor and was fitted with specially angled heads, sizable intakes, aluminum pistons, and forged steel rods. If that sounds like full-race to you, that's exactly

The Boss 351 was a single-year model — 1971.

The Boss 351 engine was rated at 330 horsepower.

what it was. The Boss 351 cost a hefty $4124, the most expensive Mustang that model year.

Appearance-wise, the Boss 351 looked considerably different from the Boss 302. The body style was completely changed for 1971, giving the Boss 351 a more subtle look than the rakish 302 of 1969 and 1970. The side stripe was still there, but it ran almost the complete length of the body before turning down through the marker light on the front fender. Production of the Boss 351 totalled a minimal 1806—no wonder the middle member of the Boss family is so rare.

Now for the King, the Big Guy—the Boss 429. No flashy striping announced the entrance of this magnificent muscle; the Boss 429 decal on the front fenders said all that needed to be said.

Ask anybody who ever owned one of these maulers and they will quickly affirm that the reported 375 horsepower was a joke. The figure was probably closer to 500, and the Boss 429 could well have held the most powerful engine ever produced. It wasn't quite as fast, though, as the 428 Cobra Jet-powered Mustangs.

Production of the Boss 429 was also very limited, with only 859 produced in 1969 and 499 in 1970. The numbers were enough, though, to qualify the engine for NASCAR oval and NHRA drag racing. The actual racing Boss 429s were assembled by Ford's racing arm, Kar Kraft, which completed the cars in its Brighton, Michigan, production facility. All Boss 429s were designated with a KK 429 NASCAR number.

The 1970 Boss 429's appearance was understated compared to its potential.

The 429 motor (which carried a Z engine code) featured a 4.36-inch bore and 3.59-inch stroke with 11.3:1 compression. Other performance goodies included forged steel rods, aluminum intake manifold and heads, and forged

Aren't you glad you didn't get the job of shoehorning the Boss 429 engine into the Mustang?

aluminum pistons. The remainder of the power train included the four-speed top-loader transmission, competition suspension, and Traction Lock rear end. And if you wanted more, there were options such as an oil cooler, Ram Air hood, and front spoiler. A distinctive feature of the Boss 429 was its headers, which hung far below the body lines and looked as if they might scrape the ground. It took a real squeeze job to shoehorn the giant powerplant into the Mustang's engine compartment.

Mustang 351 HO

Another interesting Mustang variant is the 351 HO Mustang. Never heard of it? Even the most informed Ford expert might have trouble with this 1971 mutation. Here's the story: With the Boss family gone, there were no more big-horsepower machines, but Ford wanted to hang on to its past image, even if it didn't have the horsepower to do it.

The 351 HO engine was rated at a very conservative 275 horses, but it should be remembered that during this time period, figures were quoted in net horsepower, which resulted in reduced numbers from the gross horsepower citations used previously. The lower numbers also looked better to insurance companies, which were notorious for adding surcharges to the premiums for the big-horsepower machines of the time.

Even though this was the beginning of the end for 1960s-type muscle cars, the 351 HO surprisingly contained a lot of high-performance components such as aluminum pistons and forged rods. Production numbers are unknown, but they must be minuscule since the variant was produced for only a few months.

Shelby GT-350 and GT-500

In the early 1960s, the scene was set for Ford involvement in racing. Lee Iacocca was well aware of the sales benefits that could be derived from success on the racetrack. From that motivation, the Mustang's association with Shelby American was born. The GT-350, a modification of the 289 Hi-Po Mustang, was the first product of that association.

The Shelby changes were considerable, with the already-potent Hi-Po kicked up from 271 horses to an earth-shaking 306. To accomplish this power increase, Shelby added an aluminum intake, special Y headers and a 715 CFM Holley carb, replacing the stock Hi-Po 480 CFM Autolite carburetor. Special suspension modifications precisely identified this machine as a Shelby.

Also involved in the Shelby GT-350 conversion were a Borg-Warner T-10 transmission, Koni shock absorbers, and a nine-inch modified Galaxie rear end. An additional "export" brace was added under the hood along with a quicker steering ratio. Finally, a front sway bar was added. We're talking a real race machine here, right off the showroom floor. A total of 562 GT-350s were built in the inaugural 1965 model year.

The GT-350 was effectively a two-seater, with the back seat area the resting place for the spare tire. After all, who ever heard of a four-seat racing machine? A

The Shelby modifications made an already great car look even flashier. This one's a 1966 GT-350.

special housing on the dash contained the 8000-rpm tachometer and oil pressure gauge. The GT-350 didn't come cheap, with a sticker price of $4547 — more than the base price of a brand-new Corvette Sting Ray.

There was also a modified GT-350 for even higher performance. The so-called R versions were built strictly for racing purposes and incorporated such

Among Shelby's modifications to the Mustang engine compartment was a special brace.

changes as front ducting for brake cooling, a quick-release 34-gallon gas tank, and plexiglass windows. Even the already potent powerplant was refined further, resulting in at least a 50-horsepower increase.

Whereas all 1965 GT-350s were painted white, it was possible to acquire the 1966 Shelby Mustang in four colors. An interesting addition for the model year was the optional Paxton supercharger. This $670 option increased power under the hood by as much as 40 to 50 percent—as if you really needed it. Changes to accommodate the supercharger included a rejetted 460 CFM carburetor and a special air cleaner and fuel pump.

It's not surprising to learn that these Paxton-equipped models are of great interest to collectors and are bringing the highest prices. The supercharged Shelbys were available through 1968. Research shows that about 500 of the units were built for 1966, with lower numbers for 1967 and 1968.

You could even rent a GT-350 in 1966 at your neighborhood Hertz Rent-A-Car. Hertz bought 936 cars for its ''Rent A Racer'' promotion. The program was a great success, and the cars themselves were designated GT-350H. Most of the cars were painted black with the characteristic striping in gold, and most, if not all, were equipped with automatic transmissions. You had better believe that many of these cars were thoroughly thrashed at neighborhood dragstrips. Among the early Shelbys, the H-models are highly sought-after collectibles.

The Paxton supercharger was an option from 1966 to 1968 on GT-350s. It was worth a bounding 40 percent increase in horsepower. This early prototype unit is owned by Steve Yates of Nashville, Indiana.

Major styling changes punctuated the 1967 GT-350, with a redesigned fiberglass hood, grille-mounted driving lights, hood pins, rear deck spoiler, and functional coding scoops on the sides. The '67s also reportedly used stock 289 Hi-Po powerplants instead of the previous 306-hp version.

But the big news for 1967 was the introduction of the new GT-500 Shelby Mustang. The larger '67 Mustang had the room to mount a larger power plant, and Shelby made use of that extra space by stuffing in a 428-cubic-inch engine. Hooked up with two four-barrels, it was capable of 355 horsepower. Both a four-speed and automatic were offered in the GT-500. In addition, a very few of the initial GT-500s (probably about four dozen) were built with the 427 powerplant, making them very attractive (and expensive) on the 1990s market.

Things started to change for the Shelby in 1968. First, the production location for the cars was moved from California to Michigan. Then Ford's basic 302-cubic-inch, 250-horsepower engine became the stock powerplant for the GT-350, certainly a far cry from the brutish 306-hp engines of the earlier models. For the GT-500s, the standard powerplant became the 360-hp version of the 428 police interceptor engine, fed by a 715 CFM Holley carburetor.

Later in the 1968 model year, the GT-500 was fitted with the 428 Cobra Jet engine, causing a designation change for the model. The GT-500KR — KR stood for King of the Road, an appropriate nomenclature — also required some strengthening in the engine compartment. The update was announced by the

A limited number of the 1967 Shelby 427 powerplants were equipped with this rare Weber carb induction setup.

Shelby's 1968 GT-500 did the GT-350 one step better with the 428-cubic-inch powerplant. The 335 horses were helped along by twin carbs.

addition of KR to the GT-500 in the side striping, along with Cobra Jet 428 nameplates.

Even more standard Mustang hardware was used in the 1969 Shelbys, with the GT-350s upgraded from the 302 to the 351-cubic-inch, 290-horsepower engine. To hide its stock roots, the engine was detailed with aluminum valve covers and intake manifold. The GT-500 used the same 428 Cobra Jet power-plant for 1969, similarly detailed as the GT-350, although the advertised horse-power had been downgraded to 335. The Shelbys were also now produced on the standard Mustang production lines. A total of 1279 GT-350s and 1871 GT-500s were produced in 1968, and they are extremely desirable to muscle fans.

Sadly, 1970 was the final year for the dashing Shelby Mustangs. But these weren't even really 1970 models, just extras from 1969 production. The official production number for 1970 is just 789. With only slight trim differences, the 1970 Shelbys were basically identical to the 1969s. It was a depressing end to a great era of performance.

Shelby Cobra

Was it a sports car or a muscle car? The Shelby Cobra was both, and today it's one of the most sought-after collector cars in the world, muscle machine or not.

It all started in 1962, when one Carroll Shelby decided he wanted to design and build a car that looked like a racer but could also be driven on the streets.

The result was a machine that carried roots from both sides of the Atlantic. Shelby took the classic body style and chassis of the AC Ace and stuffed its little engine compartment with Ford power in the form of a peppy 260-cubic-inch, 260-horsepower small-block power plant. He beefed up the suspension with

Larry Acheson's magnificent 1964 289 Cobra is one of the finest in the land.

special leaf springs. The initial Shelby Cobra was a rocket, with quarter-mile performance in the 12-second range. These first 260 Cobras were produced in extremely low numbers and are very rare.

Externally, the 1963 Cobras looked like the '62s, but the 260 was gone, replaced by two versions of the reliable 289 engine. A race version of the power-plant was worth almost 400 horses, while even the standard 271-hp version provided the new Cobra with impressive performance. With only minor refinements, the Cobra stayed pretty much the same for 1964.

The next year, 1965, would be the last one for the small-block 289 in the Cobra; there would also be some other performance-enhancing changes. Two special racing packages for the Cobra were offered, the Slalom Snake and Dragon Snake models.

But the big—literally—news for 1965 was the midyear introduction of the monstrous 427 mill—really monstrous when one considers the small size of the Cobra. Think about this: The 427 Cobra could reportedly go from 0 to 100 miles per hour and back to a stop in just over 13 seconds! Although it looked similar to the 289 version, the 427 Cobra required an all-new body to accommodate the new powerplant; overall length, for example, increased by five inches.

The 425-horse version of the Cobra's 427-cubic-inch engine was equipped with twin four-barrels that gave 0-to-60 performance in just over four seconds. Was this the ultimate muscle car? Many think so.

Yet another engine change came near the end of the Cobra's production run. Ford's 428 engine (rated at about 400 horsepower) was substituted for the 427. What's 25 horses among friends, that being the difference between the two powerplants? With either big-block Ford, though, there was more horsepower than most drivers could handle.

Unfortunately, 1967 was the final year for the classic Cobra. The 428 engine, because of its much better drivability, was the engine of choice for this final year.

The value of the 427 Cobra — and, to a lesser degree, the 428-powered machines — has reached astronomical heights. The trend for these interesting European-American combinations for the 1990s will do nothing but continue to move in a straight-up direction — most likely into seven figures.

Fast Fairlanes: GT, Torino, Cobra, and Super Cobra Jet

One might question the classification of Ford's midsize family cruiser, the Fairlane, as a muscle car. But taking into account the many high-performance variants that were spun off the Fairlane nameplate during the late 1960s and early 1970s, its muscle credentials are impeccable. Muscle Fairlane variants include the Torino, the Cobra, the sleek Talladega, and the bullish Thunderbolt drag cars.

The Fairlane was a late starter in the muscle wars, not really joining the fray until 1966. In 1965, the indications of coming performance were there, but the biggest power plant in the midsized Ford was the 289 Hi-Po — no match for the competition. The need for a big-block powerplant was obvious, and it came in 1966.

The savior engine for the Fairlane was Ford's potent 390-cubic-inch mill in its four-barrel 335-horse version. There were also 315 and 265-hp versions of the 390 available, but for the performance-minded, the 335-horse version was the way to go. But the ultimate powerplant (there were only 71 produced) was the awesome 427-cubic-inch, 425-hp screamer proven in Ford's racing activities.

New body styling for 1966, and new models called the 500 and 500 XL, were combined with a GT option that really set off the looks of the Fairlane. It now had the looks and power to compete with anybody.

The 1967 Fairlane stayed pretty much the same in appearance, with only slight updating. The 427-powered machines were produced in greater numbers, using to great advantage the success enjoyed by the powerplant in NASCAR competition. There were both 420- and 425-horse versions of the 427. Without a doubt, the 427-powered '66 and '67 Fairlanes are two cars certain to escalate in value. There were also several variations of the 390 engine still on the 1967 option ticket, with a 320-horse version being the top power-producer.

Enter a new Fairlane name for 1968 — the Torino, which would carry on the Fairlane performance image in great fashion in the years to follow. There was a brand-new body style to go along with the new name, but the 427 would only be available during the first part of the model year. But never fear, an able replacement was ready with the 325-hp version of the 428 Cobra Jet. A 265-horse 390 was the top version of that venerable powerplant.

The new fastback body style cheated the wind and made great strides on the NASCAR tracks, as it was considerably faster than the Fairlanes of the previous year. Torinos also won both the USAC and ARCA stock car championships.

Cobra was the big name in the Fairlane line for 1969, and the body style would incorporate the 428-cubic-inch mill as the standard power plant. The Cobra was Ford's answer to Plymouth's phenomenally successful Road Runner —a stripped-down, no-frills economy blaster meant to move off the showroom floor. The model spoke of speed and performance with a blacked-out grille, hood pins, and wheel well moldings, and was available in both fastback and formal hardtop body styles. But there was a lot more for the Fairlane in this last year of the performance decade.

The Torino officially remained the top of the Fairlane line, but the model would not carry a muscle powerplant like its Cobra brother. The standard Torino power plant was only a 302, but things changed for this model the following year, making it one of the most desirable Ford muscle machines.

Also of interest to muscle fans during 1969 were certain versions of the GT, which could be acquired with a 290-horse, 351 Windsor powerplant, the 320-horse, 390-cubic-inch engine, and the most desirable 428 pounder. At the start of the 1990s, many of these cars are still available for reasonable prices—but you can bet they won't be for long.

In 1970, a combination of the Cobra and Torino nameplates formed the new Torino Cobra, one of the most awesome Ford muscle machines ever. The fact that they carried the then-new 429-cubic-inch powerplant makes the 7,675 produced very desirable today.

A little explanation is required on the different versions of the model. The top of the Torino Cobra line mounted the so-called Super Cobra Jet 429 power-

This 1969 fastback Cobra carries the Super Cobra Jet version of the 428 powerplant. The horsepower was advertised at a ridiculously low 335. Roger Hoffman of Dayton, Ohio, owns this beautiful example.

The Super Cobra Jet version of the 428 Ford powerplant created 440 foot-pounds of torque at 3400 rpm and was capable of 14-second performance in the quarter.

In 1970, Ford introduced a new Torino along with several versions of the new 429 engine. This Torino GT Cobra Jet belongs to Kent Von Behren of Miamisburg, Ohio, and carries the coveted Super Cobra Jet version of the powerplant, capable of an advertised 375 horsepower—a killer on the dragstrip.

Bill Draper of Tinley Park, Illinois, owns one of the best 1970 Torinos in the nation. It was one of 7675 built that model year, and one of considerably fewer that carried the performance-enhancing Drag Pack option.

plant, which punched out 375 horses. Carrying a 780 CFM four-barrel Holley carb, the SCJ also sported a high-rise manifold, forged aluminum pistons, a four-bolt main block, and a unique engine oil cooler.

Next down the line was the 429 Cobra Jet Ram Air version, which carried a functional shaker hood scoop and produced 370 horsepower. The 429 Cobra engine was next down, with a Rochester four-barrel carb, cast-aluminum pistons, and 11:1 compression ratio; it was also rated at 370 horses. The bottom of the line was certainly no slouch, as the 429 Thunderjet engine was rated at only 10 horses less than its next biggest brother.

A serious performance package called the Drag Pack was also available with the Torino Cobra. Included in the option were a special oil cooler, high-performance engine parts, and a 4.30 Detroit Locker rear end.

Just as quickly as it arrived, the performance in the Fairlane line started to fade away. For 1971, the final year for the magnificent 429 Cobra Jet, the big-block still kept its horsepower rating at 370. Available versions of the 351 Cleveland engine provided horsepower ratings of 285 and 240. Needless to say, the 429 Torino Cobras will draw big dollars this decade, but the 351 machines are also starting to generate considerable collector interest.

For 1972, the 429 perked on only two barrels of carburetor and the horsepower was down to a paltry 205 net. A weak 400 engine was capable of only 163 horses. Surprisingly, the third-biggest engine in terms of cubic inches, a 351 Cleveland, put out 248 net horsepower.

The muscle era was over by 1972, but a number of interesting Fairlane muscle machines will keep them under examination for many years to come.

Falcon

The Falcon in a muscle car book? Must be some kind of a misprint. Isn't the Falcon that boxy little underpowered car at the bottom of any performance chart?

Well, that's where most people remember it, but the Falcon did have its time in the spotlight with some surprising high-performance versions. The idea of a potent powerplant in the utilitarian little Falcon makes these unique machines very interesting collectibles.

Up until 1964, the 260 V-8 was the biggest engine that could be had in the Falcon. In 1965, the 289 became available, and by 1967, the 225-horsepower, four-barrel 289 was a Falcon option — still far behind the 400-plus-cubic-inch mills installed in its Fairlane and Galaxie brothers. In 1968, the Falcon got another power boost with the addition of a 302-cubic-inch motor — not a bad performer, and capable of providing embarrassment to some other brands on occasion. Imagine getting beat at the light by a Falcon!

But the Falcon's final year, 1970, would be its finest from a performance aspect. No longer a separate model in its own right, the Falcon was now just a nameplate on a low-line stripper version of the intermediate Fairlane/Torino. But surprise, surprise! It was possible to order a 429 Cobra Jet or a 429 Super Cobra Jet engine in the 1970½ model. There were also a limited number of 351 Cobra Jet versions built. Needless to say, these machines are very rare and cause a lot of excitement whenever one is located. It's still tough to get used to seeing the Falcon name on the rear fender with a big-block engine sitting up front. Behold the Ford Falcon: the unsuspected little muscle car.

The 429 Super Cobra Jet was the top to the line for 1971. The engine carried a giant 780 CFM carburetor and aluminum forged pistons.

Now, here's a rare bird. The 1970½ Falcon was a real surprise with both the 429 and 351 Cobra Jet powerplants available. The sheet metal was from the Torino.

Many would argue that a haulin' 351 Cobra Jet engine could be ordered with the Falcon, but in 1970, it was definitely possible.

Galaxie

Mention the name Ford Galaxie and visions of a family luxury sedan come to mind. But during the early 1960s, the Galaxie was packing some high-perform-ance power plants even before the term muscle car was invented.

Often overlooked as one of the first Ford muscle cars is the 1961 Galaxie, carrying the triple-carbed 401-horsepower, 390-cubic-inch powerplant.

In 1961, for example, it was possible to order a triple-carbed, 401-horsepower, 390-cubic-inch powerhouse. Those super-desirable powerplants were known as the R engines. The next-lower version of the 390 was worth 375 horses and was referred to as the Thunderbird Special 390. There was also a 300-horse version of the 390. The 352 high-performance engine was downgraded for 1961 to only 220 horses—a considerable drop from the previous year.

The 390-cubic-inch Thunderbird Special engine was available with three deuces.

The big Galaxie story for 1962 was twofold, with the introduction of the classy 500XL body style and the thunderous 406 engine. One version of the new 406 produced 385 horses (with a four-barrel), while a three-two-barrel carb setup was worth 405 ponies. Either engine is considered very desirable in the 1990s, and the numbers remaining are small.

Another big kick in the pants came in 1963, when Ford introduced its famous 427 in the Galaxie 500 and 500XL. Without a doubt, these cars are considered the best of the early 1960s Fords. Two versions of the 427 were available, the twin-carbed version putting out 425 horses while 410 came from the triple-carbed 427. A huge performance year for Ford, 1963 also saw two versions of the 406 engine. Down the horsepower family tree could also be found the 390 and 352 engines. Galaxies, not surprisingly, were dominant in NASCAR competition that year.

The 427 was around again in 1964, with the Thunderbird 427 again producing 425 horses with a pair of Holley four-barrel carbs. The three-two version was again rated at 410 horses. Then it was down again to the 390 engine (300-hp) and the 352 mill (250-hp).

Changes in the oiling system of the 427 were the big change in 1965, with the famous engine moving to the side-oiler style. The race version of this powerplant was capable of well over 600 horsepower; the street version made 425 horses and a stump-pulling 480 foot-pounds of torque. That year, only the

The awesome 427 powerplant was first available in 1963, in both the twin-carb version shown here and a single-carb version.

In 1966, the 428 engine was available in the Galaxie; it carried the 7 Liter designation on the front quarter.

twin-carbed version was available. The 390 and 352-cubic-inch engines were also available with the same ratings as in 1964.

A new 428 monster mill was available for the Galaxie in 1966, even though the 427 was still around. To avoid confusion, the two engines were named 7-Liter Cobra (427) and Thunderbird 7-Liter (428). These were among the first

The 1966 428 was rated at 345 horses — certainly no match for the 427s, which were being phased out at the time.

metric engine designations used by an American carmaker. The 428 was no match in horsepower to the old tried-and-true 427, with only 345 horsepower compared to 425.

The 427 high-performance version made its last appearance in 1967, but in 1968 came the Q-code 427 Cobra V-8, with 390 horses in its top version. The Cobra was replaced during the model year with the Thunderbird 428 power-plant, rated at 340 horses. Two versions of the venerable 390 now produced 315 and 265 horsepower.

The 360-horse version of the 429-cubic inch N-code four-barrel engine was the top power package for 1969, followed by a two-barrel version (Code K) worth 320 horses. The 390 would also carry just a single two-barrel this year, with the power rating downgraded to only 265 horses. In its first year, the 351 Windsor H code engine kicked out 250 horses. The 351W would be heard from again in muscle machines in the coming years.

Maybe the Galaxie will be remembered by most as a 1960s luxury machine, but for those in the know, it will be remembered for those thundering 406, 427, and 428-cubic-inch powerplants that could stand up to anybody during the performance years.

MERCURY DIVISION
Comet Cyclone

In 1964, the little, underpowered Mercury Comet took on some punch and style with the introduction of the Cyclone nameplate. It had no big-block, like some of the competition of the time, but it was still plenty to talk about. Ford's 289-cubic-inch mill with 210 horses was the standard engine for this machine; the super-potent Hi-Po 289 was also on the option list. Find one of those and you've got one valuable Cyclone. "Under the hood, a whiplash of surging power" was how Mercury advertisements described the Cyclone combinations.

Appearance options on the first Cyclone included a spoked steering wheel, bucket seats, and chromed engine parts. That first year, 7454 cars were sold.

Little change was evident for the 1965 Cyclone, although the two-barrel 289 engine's horsepower dropped 10 to 200. With only slightly over 2900 pounds to push, this made for a fairly peppy machine even if it did only have a two-barrel perking. The four-barrel version of the 289, known as the Super Cyclone engine, was capable of 225 horses. For the first time, the 1965 Cyclone offered several performance options, including a handling package, special fan, and a Power Transfer rear axle. By year's end, 12,347 had been sold.

Big numbers hit the completely restyled Cyclone in 1966 with the introduction of Ford's potent 390-cubic-inch powerplant in both two and four-barrel carb versions. Horsepower ratings were 265 and 275, respectively. A killer 335-horse version was standard with the GT option. The GT was a distinctive looker with stripes, scoops, and other performance options. A total of 24,164 Cyclones of all styles were sold that year.

The 390 powerplant was still the top Cyclone engine for 1967, but its horsepower rating had dropped slightly to 320 for the top version. Again, this

The 390 powerplant was introduced to the Comet in 1966. This Cyclone GT carries the 335-horse option.

biggest engine came with the GT package in one racy-looking machine. The two-barrel version of the 390 was capable of 270 horses, and there was also a new 280-cubic-inch, 200-hp mill. The venerable 289 was no longer available. Sales were also way down with only 6910 built.

The '68 Cyclone (the Comet name had been dropped) had one big thing going for it: It was the fastest car of the year—at least according to a world-record run of 189.22 miles per hour at Daytona. The Cyclone's powerplant choices were numerous. At the bottom of the horsepower curve were two versions of the 302 powerplant with 210 (two-barrel carb) and 230 horses (four-barrel carb).

The long-standing 390 mill came in either a 265- or 335-horse version, depending again on the carburetor. Want more? It was available in '68 with the new 427 engine rated at a bone-jarring 390 horses. Also on tap was the 428 engine, but its horsepower rating fell far below the 427's, with only 335. All of these big-cube versions of the Cyclone should be considered highly desirable muscle cars, but since a total of only 13,628 were built that year, not many are around anymore.

CJ was the new nameplate for the 1969 Cyclone, a model that featured a blacked-out grille, special emblems, a 3.50 rear axle ratio, handling package, chrome engine parts, and dual exhausts. For the Cyclone CJ, the 428-cubic-inch, 335-hp engine was standard, but there was more, much more.

The 390-horsepower version of the 427 was still available, but now a 429 engine showed 335 horses in four-barrel configuration. Also available were a 220-hp 302 motor, a pair of 351 engines with 250 and 290 horses, and finally, a 320-horse version of the 390 engine. Considering the huge engine selection, the Cobra Jet Cyclone sold rather poorly—only 3,261.

The 1969 Cyclone CJ carried the 428-cubic-inch powerplant as its standard engine.

The Cyclone line was completely restyled for 1970, with three versions available. The standard model carried the 429 Thunder Jet powerplant, or you could choose the Cyclone GT or the winged Cyclone Spoiler.

As in 1969, a wide variety of muscle engines was available. There were 220 (two-barrel), 250, and 300-horse versions of the 351, along with versions of the

The 1969 Cyclone CJ 428 was worth 335 horsepower and will make this model a great catch in the years to come.

Pete Bates has a lot to be proud of with his 1970 Cyclone GT. It has the very desirable 429-cubic-inch, 360-horse powerplant.

versatile 429 mill rated at 360, 370, and 375 horsepower. There was also a limited special-order Boss 429 engine option; these were extremely rare, and as of this writing, none have been located.

The king of the fleet was the Cyclone Spoiler, which carried the sleek look of a race car. The model featured both front and rear spoilers, body racing stripes, scooped hood, racing mirrors, and a competition racing package. Both the Cobra Jet and Super Cobra Jet versions of the 429 engine were available with the Spoiler. This highly sought-after machine will escalate in value with each passing year.

A number of these '70 Cyclone machines should still be around, as the basic Cyclone model sold 1695 copies, the GT 10,170, and the Spoiler 1631. Considering the appearance and performance of these models, the 1970 Cyclones should continue to be a high-interest model for many years. They certainly haven't received the attention of their Torino and Fairlane brothers, so perhaps you can still get in on the ground floor of the Cyclone's increasing popularity.

The beginning of the end began for the Cyclone in 1971, when it became part of the Montego line. There were the Montego Cyclone, the Montego Cyclone GT, and the Montego Cyclone Spoiler. These are very rare Mercury muscle machines, with only 444, 2287, and 353 produced, respectively.

Other muscle-type engines that could be ordered with the '71 Cyclone included a 210-horse 302 and 240- and 285-horse versions of the 351 engine.

This magnificent Mercury marked its last year in 1971. The Cyclone was one of the casualties of nosediving cubic inches and horsepower.

Cougar XR-7 and Eliminator

The year was 1967 and Mercury badly needed a pony car to compete in this hot new market. Its answer came in the form of the Cougar, a sporty coupe that in many ways was nothing more (or less) than a restyled and upgraded Mustang.

The super-rare 1968 GT-E was the ultimate Cougar muscle car. There were versions with both the 427 and 428 powerplants. Only 602 were constructed, and Wayne Richardson of Xenia, Ohio, has one of the 427 versions. In its younger days, Wayne was able to push his GT-E to 13.7-second quarters.

That first Cougar was a flashy devil, though, with its triple sequential rear turn signals and overall slinky look.

The standard powerplant was a run-of-the-mill 200-hp 289, but much more was available in the GT version of the Cougar. A pavement-pounding 390-cubic-inch, 320-horse engine really turned the Cougar GT into a rocket. A Holley four-barrel, 10.5 : 1 compression ratio pistons, and low-restriction exhausts were among the goodies that made this engine one of the best.

But there was even more for this first year. Continuing to play the catch-up game, Mercury introduced a new luxury model called the XR-7. Walnut and leather were the keynotes of this beauty's interior, and 27,221 were constructed.

The '68 XR-7 looked about the same as the '67, but carried a number of muscle powerplant options, all of which are growing in popularity in the early 1990s. Two versions of the 390-cubic-inch engine were available with 280- and 325-horsepower ratings. There was also an optional 428-cube engine available.

An interesting one-year-only Cougar model was the so-called GT-E. This performance version started out the year with the 427 side-oiler engine, which was replaced mid-year with the 428 Cobra Jet. The GT-E didn't exactly overrun the showrooms; only 602 were sold. Well over half—358 to be exact—carried the 427 engine. Few of these cars have been located, but they are certainly very interesting and little-known Ford muscle cars. A good investment? You bet.

The standard XR-7 in 1969 carried more of the good stuff. In addition to the 428 Cobra Jet Ram Air 335-horse engine, there was also available as an option (theoretically) the killer 429-cubic-inch four-barrel 360-horse humper, although none have been documented. The Cougar engine parade also included 302-, 351-, and 390-cube engines.

One of the most attractive muscle Cougars was introduced in 1969, the sporty Cougar Eliminator. A number of engines were available in the Eliminator, with a 290-horse version of the 351, the standard powerplant. Other Eliminator

Look close — you're not likely to see a 427 Cougar every day.

The flashy Cougar Eliminator sported complete body-length stripes, rear spoiler, and block Eliminator lettering on the rear quarter — it's one sharp little muscle machine. Mike Besecker is the owner of this beautiful yellow 1970 model.

engine options included the Boss 302 and two versions of the 428. Only 2411 Eliminators were built in 1969, the first of its two years. You still see one every now and then, and the nice thing about these somewhat forgotten muscle cars is that they are often reasonable in price. (That situation, though, probably won't last much longer.)

Even fewer of the flashy Eliminators were constructed in 1970 — 2200, to be exact. The engine options for this year were again the Boss 302 (290 horses), the 351 Cleveland (300 horses) and the 428 Cobra Jet (335 horses). A special Competition Handling Package came as standard equipment on the Eliminators both years and drew positive reaction from the magazine road tests of the car.

As was the case with most models of any manufacturer, these powerful engines were also available in the plain-Jane versions of the Cougar. Even though it's not documented, there are undoubtedly some stripped-down Cougars running around with 428 Cobra Jets under their hoods. To many collectors, these cars are just as appealing from a muscle point of view as the fancy Eliminators and XR-7s.

By 1971, the Eliminator was gone, but certainly not the performance aspects of the Cougar. Available with the XR-7 and other Cougars were the awesome 429 Super Cobra Jet with a 370-horse rating and the 285-horse 351 mill. A GT package provided the performance equipment and looks to go along with the power under the hood, including a high-ratio rear axle, high-performance suspension system, hood scoop, and racing mirrors. Over 27,000 XR-7s were sold that year.

Big power was available again in the Cougar for 1972, but the downward trend was under way. The 351 engine was now down 23 horses from the previous year, while the big-blocks had departed completely. A Cobra Jet version of the 351 engine was listed as capable of 266 horses, and came with a competition suspension system and dual exhausts. The 1972 XR-7 also offered a GT package similar to the previous year. An almost identical number of XR-7s were sold this year.

Sales continued to be brisk for the XR-7 in 1973, but the cars certainly weren't being bought for their muscle during this time period. The 351 Cobra Jet engine was still the king, with a 264-horse rating for 1974 and 1975. Even though both a 460-cubic-inch, 220-horse powerplant and a 400-cube, 170-horse engine would be introduced, they certainly couldn't hold a candle to the killer engines of the earlier years.

It was over for the muscle Cougars, but through the years some very collectible machines were produced. In several cases, their attraction hasn't really caught on yet, and many of these Cougar-based machines can be purchased at very reasonable prices. They certainly deserve a look in the 1990s.

FORDS'S FLYERS: FORD TALLADEGA AND MERCURY SPOILER

The last years of the 1960s was a time of huge racing exposure for all the automakers, including Ford. It was a great time for the Blue Oval brand, with the

Ford Talladega and Mercury Cyclone II blowing away the formidable Chrysler competition in NASCAR long-oval-track competition. In 1969, the Talladega racked up 11 wins and the Spoiler II four in tracks exceeding one mile. In 1970, these Ford factory racers were still very dominant, with eight long-track victories.

In order to race these slippery limited-edition models, NASCAR mandated that at least 500 of each be built for regular highway use and offered for sale to the public. For the Talladega, production totaled 754 cars, while the Cyclone Spoiler II saw an estimated 519 produced. Both were built for only the 1969 model year.

The Talladega was actually a Torino, even though it didn't look much like one, with its special extended fenders and the grille pulled flush and dropped lower. It was about six inches longer than the standard Fairlane, with aerodynamics dictating that the roofline be about an inch lower.

If the driver was looking for luxury in the Talladega, he could forget it. The car was built in a plain-Jane motif with a cheap black bench-seat interior and an exterior available in only three colors. Options were also kept to a minimum. Three small identifiers (aside from the obvious front end) marked this Torino as a Talladega. A large T appeared on the top of the fake gas cap, a small rectangular nameplate on the top of the door sheetmetal just below the window opening contained a Ford emblem and a T, and the Talladega name was blocked out on the inside of each door panel. Built on the Torino frame, the models carried staggered rear shocks and heavy-duty suspension. Other standard features included blacked-out hood and rear panel, full body trim, and re-rolled rocker panels.

The Talladega's power was up to its looks, with a 428-cubic-inch, 335-horsepower Cobra Jet engine. The mill wore a huge 735 CFM carb topside and was capable of 440 foot-pounds of torque. The Talladega is a muscle car collectible of the first order.

Not to be left out, the Mercury Division released the Cyclone Spoiler II to also prowl the NASCAR speedways. But the Cyclone wasn't an exact copy of

The Talladega was built to qualify for NASCAR racing. In 1969, the Talladega saw the checkered flag 11 times. The 428 Cobra Jet powerplant with 335 horses provided the punch.

Mercury's answer to the Talladega was the Cyclone Spoiler II. Cale Yarborough and Dan Gurney versions of the model each wore the famous drivers' scripted names.

its Talladega kin; there were small changes that gave it slightly improved aerodynamics.

There were actually two versions of the Spoiler II. The Cale Yarborough model came in red and white, while the Dan Gurney version was blue and white. The scripted signature of each famous driver was carried on the front fenders.

Like the Talladega, the Spoiler II sported considerable aerodynamic modifications to the front end. The front bumper was specially built by Detroit Steel Tubing, which modified a Fairlane rear bumper to perform the front-facing duties. The rocker panels were also re-rolled for improved aerodynamics.

The biggest differences between the street versions of Ford's swift pair, though, were under the hood. The Mercury Spoiler carried the 351-cubic-inch Windsor instead of the Talladega's 428CJ; 290 horses were residing in the Spoiler's mill, which was hooked to an FMX automatic transmission and a nine-inch rear end.

These racy machines are very rare, but a few of them are still around. With their extensively modified front ends, the cars would be very difficult to duplicate. They are real collectors' items, and the opportunity to acquire one should never be passed up.

CHAPTER IV

Chrysler Muscle Cars

CHRYSLER REALLY STARTED THE MUSCLE CAR CRAZE IN THE 1950s WITH THE big-horsepower versions of the Chrysler 300. After that came the 413 and 426 Max Wedge-powered Plymouths and Dodges, and later still, of course, the legendary 426 Hemis. Each division of the company designed and marketed its own family of muscle machines. The Chrysler (or MOPAR, as it's also known) engine family, though, was basically common to both Plymouth and Dodge brands—and what a powerful bunch they were. The immortal 426 Hemi was the king of the mountain, with a whopping 425 horses and unbelievable low-end torque. It was available—at a sizable premium—in most Plymouth and Dodge models. Today, any Chrysler with a Hemi under the hood is at the top of the value chart. In all, slightly fewer than 10,000 street Hemis of all models were built during the performance years of 1965 to 1971.

To many muscle enthusiasts, the 440-cubic-inch three-two-barrel powerplants are just as desirable and collectible. There was also a four-barrel carb version of the potent 440. More plentiful still were strong four-barrel versions of the 383- and 340-cubic-inch engines. A special three-carb version of the 340 was also available on the Dodge T/A Challenger and the Plymouth AAR 'Cuda.

Even the names of the Chrysler machines were exciting and macho-sounding. For Plymouth, there were the Barracuda, 'Cuda, Road Runner, GTX, Duster, and Superbird. The Dodge nomenclature was equally stimulating, with the Dart, Demon Charger, Challenger, Super Bee, and Daytona.

The MOPAR machines were also among the most eye-catching of all muscle cars, from their attention-getting graphics to their unbelievably wild colors (would you believe bright purple?). Add all that to the swoopy race-car styling of the time period and you've got some amazing supercars that today are among the most sought-after automobiles ever built.

Although the emphasis of this chapter is on Chrysler's top-gun muscle models, it should be noted that it was also possible to acquire most of the big engines in the less-luxurious models. The Coronet, Belvedere, and Satellite models that carry the big engines are legitimate muscle cars, and, to some, are even more interesting than the top-of-the-line models.

Chrysler muscle machines are among the hot tickets for collecting in the 1990s. And the nice thing is that many of them are still around.

CHRYSLER 300

For most, the current muscle car rage applies to the mid-1960s and early 1970s time period. But for Chrysler, the muscle trend started much earlier, with the powerful Chrysler 300 series in the 1950s. The 300 story is one of big horsepower that peaked early and then was virtually dead by the time the real muscle craze began. It's appropriate, though, to look at what many consider to be the first muscle car.

The first year for the Chrysler 300 and its performance image was 1955. That was the year that the powerful machines won both the NASCAR and AAA stock car championships. A legend was born.

During its early years, the 300 served to aid in the development of the famous Hemi powerplant. The engine started out at 331 cubic inches and grew to 392 cubes before it was discontinued in 1959 in favor of the 413-cubic-inch

This 1956 354-cubic-inch, 340-horse Hemi was one of the early Chrysler 300 powerplants.

Wedge motor. The 413 proved to be a real winner for Chrysler, with a ram induction system added to the engine in 1960.

Eight ram tubes crossed horizontally over the engine and supplied the air-fuel mixture to the cylinders, rammed by sonic pulses. A supercharging effect was created by the moving column of air in the ram tubes due to the operating of the intake valves.

Two years later, the exotic induction system would be available only on the optional 405-horsepower version, with the standard engine equipped with in-line center-mounted dual quad carbs. This version was capable of 380 horses at 5200 rpm, and was officially clocked at 93 miles per hour and 15 seconds flat in the quarter-mile. Later that same year, a 300H (1962 designation) would set a flying mile national record at 179.4 miles per hour. Then Ray Brock, at the wheel of another specially prepared 300H, placed second at the NHRA Nationals at a speed of 108.4 miles per hour in a startling 12.88 seconds.

The stage was set for bigger and better things for the powerful Chrysler 300 machines, but 1962 signaled the end of high horsepower for these cars—just when things were really getting started for the recognized musclecar era. Only 558 of the H models would be produced in that final year of Chrysler 300 high-performance.

It was the beginning, though, of a decade of big power and big cubic-inch performance for Chrysler—and it all started with the Chrysler 300 machines—the first muscle cars.

The 1962 Chrysler 300 was a forerunner of the Chrysler muscle to come. George Cone of Crystal Lakes, Illinois owns this powerful 380-horse machine.

413 AND 426 MAX WEDGE

The Chrysler 413-cubic-inch powerplant is currently not as well known as its later 383, 440, and Hemi running mates, but during its early days it was one of the real killer engines. Its roots reach deep into Chrysler's drag-racing days.

The 413 first appeared in the Chrysler line in 1959. Two years later it would be available in both Plymouths and Dodges. At the time of its introduction, its power was impressive at 400 horses and 465 foot-pounds of torque. The 413s were also equipped with dual carbs.

The famous Max Wedge nomenclature began in 1962 and the powerplant quickly proved itself on the nation's dragstrips. The power of the new engine (rated 410 horsepower) came from its wedge-shaped combustion chambers. The same engine was known by different names in different models— Ramcharger in a Dodge and Super Streak in a Plymouth. The powerplant was topped by a pair of offset Carter 650 CFM carbs and carried TRW pistons and forged rods.

In 1963, the 413 Max Wedge had to take a backseat to an engine 13 cubes larger, the 426 Max Wedge. In fact, the Max Wedge name no longer was applied to the 413, since only milder versions of the engine were available. Both 340- and 390-horse versions were available in '63 413s, the latter with a twin-carb setup. The 413 option lasted through 1965, but the dual-carb version went by the wayside. The 426 Max Wedge II could be ordered with either 11:1 compression

The Max Wedge II 426 powerplant was capable of 415 horsepower in 1963. Note the staggered carburetor arrangement.

In 1964, the Wedge's horsepower was up to 425. The engine's last year was 1965, when it gave way to the famous 426 Hemi power plant with the same horsepower.

(415 horsepower) or 13.5:1 compression, which developed an additional 10 horses.

A year later, Chrysler called it the 425-horsepower Max Wedge III and there were even more performance improvements with larger Carter carbs and the new Tri-Y headers. A street version of the powerful engine appeared in 1964, but this was no engine for the street—as those who bought one quickly found out. The Street Wedge's last year was 1965, when it gave way to the onrushing 426 Hemi; its horsepower rating was the same 365 that it had been in 1964.

These early muscle powerplants are sometimes forgotten in the current mania for the mid-1960s and early-1970s muscle cars. But the 413 and 426 Wedges were the start of the muscle car era as we know it. And the limited number remaining will become high-dollar investments in the years to come.

DODGE DIVISION
Charger

Charger—what a great name for the sleek new machine that Dodge introduced in 1966. The name lasted through the 1974 model year and represented some of the most exciting muscle models ever to come down the line.

The initial Charger's fastback styling and trick interior were the keynotes of its design. It had four bucket seats, and the two rear ones could be folded down

The first of the Charger breed was introduced in 1966. Its revolutionary design and powerplant choices of 383 and Hemi engines made it a standout.

to form a voluminous cavern capable of hauling just about anything. It was almost like having a station wagon in a sedan body. The eye-catching dash design also had a bold new look, with four large lids containing all the needed instruments — including a 150-mile-per-hour speedometer and a 6000-rpm tachometer.

The standard engine for this first Charger was a rather sedate 318, but there was power aplenty in the engines on the option sheet. The list included the 383-cube, 325-horse engine and the untouchable 426 Hemi. Reportedly, the first 3000 383 engines were experimental models carrying a Stage III cam, hydraulic lifters, special springs, and 2¼-inch valves. Of the 37,300 Chargers built that inaugural season, only 468 carried the Hemi.

For 1967, few changes were made to the Charger's sheetmetal, but under the hood, the performance-minded buyer was offered the 440-cubic-inch, 375-horse powerplant for the first time. Sales, though, were disappointing, and only 15,788 were built. A '66 or '67 Charger with one of the Big Three powerplants today would be a great find, but they are rarely seen.

The following year, the Charger got a complete body redesign, wrap-around rear stripes and R/T badges for the top-of-the-line Charger R/T model, and performance in the 14-second category. The 383 engine was also improved for 1968 with 15 additional horsepower. Only 475 of the 17,582 R/Ts sold were Hemis.

The Charger 500 model appeared for the first and only time in 1969. With its aerodynamic trick front grille and rear window treatment, it was specially crafted for NASCAR competition. The Charger 500 could be ordered with either Magnum 440 or 426 Hemi engine. The luxurious Charger SE also made its debut this

The 426 Hemi powerplant made any MOPAR machine a desirable one, then and now.

The 440-cubic-inch powerplant remained a popular choice through the Charger performance years. This was the look of the 1971 single-carb 440 Magnum version.

The 1973 Charger was starting to move away from the sleek race car look of its earlier brothers. The 340 Magnum powerplant, in a derated version, was still available this model year.

year. For 1969, 432 Charger R/Ts — out of 18,776 produced — carried the Hemi powerplant, making these worth their weight in gold for collectors.

The 440 Six-Pack powerplant was available in the Charger for the first time in 1970, but little else changed in that model year. Competition from its new Dodge stablemate, the Challenger, might have cut into 1970 Charger sales; production was about half of 1969's, at 10,337. Only 112 were Hemi-powered.

The big news for 1971 was the transfer of the economy-racer Super Bee name from the Coronet line to the Charger. Low price and high performance were the goals of this model, which carried a 300-horse version of the 383 four-barrel and a three-speed transmission. Available on the Super Bee was the same fresh-air hood that came as standard equipment on the higher-line Charger R/T. Since both the Super Bee and R/T were available with the 440 or 426 engines, both featured heavy-duty suspension. Charger R/T sales were disappointing at only 3,118.

Performance for the Charger was on the way down for 1972, when both the long-standing R/T and the Super Bee were dropped from the line. The Charger Rallye was the new kid on the block, along with the SE. Both the 426 Hemi and 440 Six Pack had succumbed to emissions laws, with the Charger's optional performance engines becoming derated versions of the 383 and 440 four-barrel, along with a new 400-cubic-inch, 190-horsepower engine. The current value of these big-cubic-inch, low-horsepower models is considerably lower than their roaring compatriots of earlier years.

The Dodge Charger still ranks right up there in popularity with the other Chrysler muscle cars, and the big-engined models will continue to demand the big bucks in the 1990s.

Dart and Demon

This Dodge pair might bring to mind of economy rather than performance, but when equipped with the family of 340-cubic-inch powerplants (and a few rare

383-inchers), these lightweight models definitely meet any muscle car standard.

Dodge's Dart had been around since 1960, but then it could hardly qualify as any kind of muscle machine; most were built with the utilitarian Chrysler slant six engine. But a limited-production version of the 383 powerplant, dubbed the D500, was available in the Dart through 1961, when a 330-horsepower, cross-ram version was added.

In 1962, the GT Dart was available with the 361-cubic-inch mill capable of 305 horses; there was also a 305-horse two-barrel version of the 383, as well as a pounding 340-horse, 413-cubic-inch engine. Reports claim that, albeit unadvertised, a limited number of the 385-horse 413s were available in the Dart.

The Dart acquired the 273-cubic-inch V-8 worth 180 horses in 1964. The car's image was still that of a nice little family sedan, but its appearance was starting to change in a big way.

The '65 Dart GT hit the street with twin off-center body-length racing stripes, bucket seats, rocker panel vents, and other appearance options. The 273 engine was still the top powerplant for 1965, but its horsepower had been pushed up to 235. In the little 2795-pound machine, the performance was impressive with 0-to-60 times of less than 10 seconds. The formerly sedate little Dart was starting to turn people's heads.

Minor restyling was accomplished for the Dart GT in 1966, with luxury updates in the interior and Dart medallions on the rear quarter panels. But for 1967, the Dart was all-new from the ground up. The 273 engine was still the top powerplant, now carrying a 700 CFM carb. The GT version loudly announced its presence with a Dart GT emblem just forward of the front door and the 273 displacement number displayed prominently on the front fender. To match the new look came a list of available options, including suspension-system updates and a handling package. A limited number of the 280-horse versions of the 383 motor were reportedly available this year.

The GTS name was new for 1968 and a new powerplant was under the hood in the form of the 340-cubic-inch, 275-horse mill.

For 1968, the name of the game was horsepower, and the Dart was a surprising beneficiary. There was new nomenclature — GTS — to go with the new 340-cubic-inch, 275 horse powerplant, bumblebee stripes on the rear quarters, and stylish hood vents. If the 340 wasn't enough, there was also a low-production 383 available. The additional 43 cubic inches cost only $25 more than the 340. And those in the know pulled strings and got one of 80 Hurst-built 425-horsepower Hemi Darts, or one of the 50 or so 440-cubic-inch, 375-hp-powered factory drag cars, both of them rare and valuable in today's collecting market.

Although not up to the Hemi, the 383 Dart GTS could reportedly fly through the traps at just over 14 seconds, clocked at nearly 100 miles per hour. Only 1150 of the 383 models were constructed and it goes without saying that these are also highly collectible in the 1990s.

The Dart Swinger 340 was the new name for 1969. Not carrying quite the luxury of its GT and GTS brothers, the Swinger packed the 275-horse version of the 340 and announced its catchy name in its rear stripes. But if you really wanted performance, you ordered the 383 option with the GTS, which carried a 330-horsepower rating. For getting from point A to point B quickly, this machine had few equals. And again, just as the year before, Hurst modified over 500 of the 383 GTS cars with the 440 powerplant; 390 horses in that machine made it an ultimate screamer. In all, some 6700 GTSs were built in all versions.

The GTS was gone for 1970, leaving only two models carrying the Dart name — the two-door hardtop and the 340 version of the Swinger both survived the cut. Performance was still a keynote, though, with the 340-cubic-inch, 275-hp powerplant the top engine. The Swinger 340 is gaining in popularity among collectors in the 1990s, even though it doesn't carry one of the coveted big-block engines. Its appearance — with rear stripes, simulated hood scoops, and optional hood paint — makes this a real sleeper for the years to come.

A smiling little red devil with a three-pronged spear was the symbol for a new small Dodge model in 1971. Actually, the so-called Demon was just this

Vertical rear-quarter stripes really set off the 1969 Dodge Swinger.

The 340-cubic-inch, 275-horse engine was standard in the '69 Dart Swinger.

It's hard to believe that Dodge would stuff the monstrous 440 Six-Pack into the GTS, but that's where they put 375 horses in 1969.

division's version of the Plymouth Duster, which had been introduced the year before. The Swinger would fall by the wayside.

Included in the 340 Demon package, which was reportedly a high 14-second performer, were side and rear deck striping, Rallye suspension, and a floor-mounted shifter. The engine was the 275-horse version of the time-tested 340, and it proved to be a popular seller (10,098 built). Maybe that attractive $2721 sticker helped at the showroom. For some reason, Demons are quite rare these days, with only a few restorations seen at the national meets. That could change in the coming years.

An interesting dealer-installed modification was the Demon GSS model, a version produced by Grand-Spaulding Dodge. Performance was this dealer's game, as it added three Holley two-barrel carbs, aluminum valve spring retainers, and competition oil filter, oil pump, and fuel pump to the already-potent 340. Some additional interior appointments really set this unique Demon model off. For an extra $570, it could be yours.

For 1972, the Demon remained the performance machine in the Dodge mini-muscle camp, but new compression ratio reduction rules were now in place, causing a horsepower drop to 240. Appearance-wise, the model changed very little. Approximately 8700 340 Demons were produced that year. So where are they all now? Look around; perhaps you can find one for an excellent low-cost restoration.

A year later the Demon name vanished, to be replaced by the Dart Sport; 11,315 of this new model were produced, all carrying the 240-horse version of the 340 engine. A big surprise came in 1974—the middle of the downturn in engine power. The performance version of the Dart Sport was named the Dart Sport 360 to honor its 20-cubic-inch-larger power plant. We're not talking big power numbers here—only 245 horses—since the 360 carried only a two-barrel carb. But in this time period, it was the best that could be called muscle performance. A total of 3951 were built.

The Demon was only around for the 1971 and 1972 model years. The standard powerplant was the 340 and few of these machines are seen today.

This 1974 Dart Sport carries the 360-cubic-inch engine that demonstrated 230 net horses — not much by earlier standards, but the engine reversed the trend of decreasing cubic inches in the 1970s.

Super Bee

During the late 1960s, muscle cars were being turned out by all the auto manufacturers, and a majority of these machines had not only high performance but high cost as well. In fact, high-performance was beyond the pocketbook of many muscle car enthusiasts. Chrysler decided that something had to be done.

Affordable Chrysler muscle began in 1968, when Plymouth introduced the Road Runner. The stripped-down rocket was an immediate hit with the performance-minded, and it sold like crazy. Dodge quickly realized that it had to have

Debbie Clark's 1969 Super Bee demonstrates the new rear bumblebee striping, with the Super Bee character within the stripes. This particular Bee carries the top-of-the line Hemi powerplant.

something similar to the Road Runner—and in a hurry. The Coronet was selected as the model that would be converted into a lightweight muscle machine. Introduced in 1965, the Coronet had a family-car image until this amazing transformation. In late 1967 it happened, and the 1968½ Super Bee was born.

Right off the bat was the powerplant—a specially designed 383-cubic-inch engine with a greatly underrated 335 horses. Not just any 383, the Super Bee's motivation was modified with 440 Magnum heads, a newly designed cam, and a new intake manifold. The remainder of the Super Bee package included a heavy-duty four-speed, performance clutch, special suspension package, and fade-resistant brakes. Real muscle collectors, take note: Reportedly, 125 1968½ Hemi Super Bees were produced.

The Super Bee's aggressive look immediately set it off. The model was accented with the popular vertical rear stripes and the distinctive Super Bee logo with a tough little killer bee in the middle of the striping.

In 1969, the Super Bee took off in the showroom with total sales of 27,800 units. The powerful 426 Hemi mill (258 sold) provided 425 horses, but equally exciting was the 440 Six-Pack system that today is considered one of the most collectible of the Chrysler performance machines.

The Bee's Six-Pack featured a high-rise manifold and three identical two-barrel Holley carbs in a row. When all three were perking, a pavement-blistering 390 horses and 490 foot-pounds of torque were available for whatever purpose the driver had in mind. For normal driving, only the center Holley was used, but punch that pedal and you had better hold on!

In order to handle the tremendous power of the Hemi and 440, a racing-type Dana rear end was installed, along with a heavy-duty suspension package that included special shocks and front and rear sway bars.

For 1970, the Super Bee was basically unchanged, but the appreciable appearance difference had stripes coming from both the top and bottom of the rear bumblebee logo and swinging forward on the rear fenders. The 383 was again the standard powerplant, and again the 440 Six-Pack and Hemi were options. Available options included hood-mounted tachometer, rear deck wing, and a performance steering wheel. Five Scat Pack packages contained various performance and appearance items for really putting some buzz in your Bee. They didn't do much for sales, though, as only 14,137 Bees were sold in the model's third year. Only 36 were Hemi-powered.

Then, in 1971, the Super Bee lost its identity as a separate model and became an option on the Charger line. Only 4,325 Super Bees were built, with 22 Hemis and 99 Six-Pack 440s.

The next year, the Bee was put to bed for good. One of the most successful muscle cars ever was only around for four years, making it very sought-after by today's collectors due to its rarity and big-engine options.

Coronet R/T

Although the Super Bee got most of the publicity during this period, it would be negligent not to mention the Coronet, upon which the Super Bee was based. Certain versions of this model also qualify quite nicely as bona fide muscle cars.

The 1967 Coronet R/T featured a unique scoop hood and dashing styling. This particular R/T carries the 426 Hemi powerplant.

Introduced by Dodge in 1965, the Coronet was around for a lot longer than its Super Bee cousin. The monstrous Hemi was available in the Coronet officially in 1966, but it was reportedly possible to get one even earlier. One year later, the four-barreled version of the 440, capable of 375 horses, was available with the Coronet. The most desirable Coronet model was the luxury R/T version, a name that in time would be used more than the Coronet name itself. Just over 2600 R/Ts were built in 1967, with only 61 carrying the Hemi.

With 1968 R/T sales over 10,500, the model showed little change in performance. In 1969, the big change was that the R/T (and also the Super Bee) could be ordered with a new fresh-air induction system. R/Ts also picked up a

This 1969 Coronet R/T, owned by Mark Waters of Dayton, Ohio, carries the 375-horse version of the 440-cubic-inch powerplant. The model was discontinued after 1970.

lot of favorable publicity with their performance on the dragstrips, many of the cars with Hemis under their hoods. Only 107 R/Ts were built with street Hemis. Carrying R/T badges and a different rear vertical stripe, an R/T was seldom confused with a Super Bee.

In 1970, R/T sales dropped to a new low, with only 2391 sold. This was surprising, since the Super Bee continued to do well. Whatever the reason, the big brass at Chrysler decided it had seen enough and killed the Coronet.

With today's huge interest in Chrysler muscle cars, either one of these machines should be taken seriously from an investment point-of-view. Taking into account the production numbers quoted, many of these cars must be still out there waiting to be discovered.

Challenger

The Dodge Challenger almost missed the muscle car era, since its career didn't start until 1970. By that time, it had a lot of catching up to do with its competition, but the Challenger had the style and the muscle to do the job.

Muscle engines for the Challenger and Challenger SE models included a 275-horsepower version of the 340 and a 330-horse version of the 383. Moving up the performance ladder, next came the Challenger R/T, which gave the buyer the 383-cubic-inch, 335-horse engine. The necessary powertrain and suspension modifications produced the full benefit of this power.

But that was just the beginning of the Challenger performance curve, with three more optional powerplants for the buyer to consider. Two versions of the mighty 440-cubic-inch engine provided either 375 or 390 horsepower. If those didn't quite sate your power appetite, the memorable 425-hp Hemi (356 were built) made the Challenger equal to any champion with 14-second, 100+-mile-

The prize possession of Larry Bell of New Castle, Indiana, this rare machine is one of the very early 1970 Challenger R/Ts carrying a 426 Hemi.

per-hour performance in the quarter-mile. All of these high-horsepower versions are extremely hot machines among today's collectors.

To many, though, the most interesting of the '70 Challengers was the T/A model, which was built specifically to qualify the model for Trans Am racing. A total of 2399 of the T/As were built to compete with the AAR 'Cudas, Boss Mustangs, Shelbys, and Z/28 Camaros. It was a beautiful muscle machine and remains extremely valuable in today's market.

The T/A design featured a wide body-length stripe that carried an embedded T/A logo on the front fender. Just below that was the announcement of the 340 Six-Pack engine, a 290-horse three-carb version of the 340 powerplant (the only 340 engine on which the setup could be ordered). It should be noted that the actual Trans Am racing T/As used a four-barrel carb 340 destroked to 305 cubic inches.

The T/A's three carbs sat on an aluminum intake manifold with air fed through a functional scoop system. A rear spoiler, heavy-duty shocks, and front and rear sway bars made the T/A a real street performer. But the T/A, one of finest performance machines ever built by Chrysler, was only around for one year. With Chrysler's withdrawal from Trans Am racing after the 1970 season, the T/A also sadly passed away. The T/As are still occasionally seen, but they are extremely rare and expensive.

In 1971, insurance and emissions regulations started to make an impact on the muscle car scene, and the performance-choking effects hit the Challenger line with lower compression ratios on the 383 engine. The 440 and Hemi powerplants escaped the throttling, but it would be the last year for both in the Challenger line. Only 71 Hemi Challengers were built in 1971, making them a magnificent find for today's collector.

The downturn really hit hard for muscle enthusiasts in 1972. The 340 was the biggest Challenger engine option, now putting out only 240 horses. Along with the power reductions, the Challenger was also losing the racy look it had

The 1971 Challenger R/T featured this flashy double racing stripe. It was the last year for the Hemi, marking the beginning of the end for big-power engines.

when it was conceived. Big engines were no longer in, and the Hemi was one of the casualties.

For 1973, the standard powerplant was a 318, hardly a muscle car candidate; a dehorsed 340 was optional. In 1974, production of the Challenger was discontinued, ending a run of some 135,000 in five years. Today a number of the big-block versions are commanding *huge* dollars—especially the Hemi-powered machines.

PLYMOUTH DIVISION
Barracuda

The Barracuda could be called Plymouth's forgotten muscle car. Oh, sure, the later 'Cuda version of the model generated plenty of performance attention, but certain versions of the basic Barracuda built fall into the muscle car category. Let's remember them here.

The first Barracuda, in the 1964½ model year, certainly didn't look like a muscle car, and it certainly didn't have much power under the hood. In reality just a glass-fastback Valiant, the first Barracuda's biggest available engine was a 273-cubic-inch, 180-horse powerplant—not exactly what you were looking for to spark your performance fires. But things would get bigger and better in the near future.

Plymouth started first on the looks category with a sporty machine called the Formula S Barracuda in 1965, which featured a tach, sport suspension, and bolt-on wheel covers. The top engine, though, stayed the same. For 1966, the 273 was still on top, but the horsepower on this venerable motor was now rated at a healthy 235, a considerable boost. Even so, it was still difficult to call this model a muscle car, then or now.

The Barracuda was completely redesigned for 1967, and the big cubes finally arrived. The 280-horse version of the 383 was optional on the Formula S;

The 1967 Barracuda underwent a complete redesign, with the 383-cubic-inch, 280-horse power-plant available for the first time. Shown here is the similar '68 model.

1784 were built with that engine. Performance was lacking compared to the competition (high 15-second performance in the quarter), but Plymouth was working on the problem. Front fender 383 Four Barrel emblems announced what was under the hood of the '67 model. A number of other appearance and performance options were included in the Formula S package.

Four engine options were available for the model in 1968, with a hot 340 added to the stable. A brand-new engine, the 340 sported a 10.5 : 1 compression ratio, forged steel crankshaft, dual-point ignition, and extremely large valves. The quoted 275 factory horsepower was evidently an understatement, since these cars were capable of 14-second quarter-mile performances. A pair of 340-S emblems on the hood announced the engine selection.

But attention was also being paid to upgrading the 383 power plant, with a 20-horse increase to 300. A few Barracudas were even modified to accept the 426 Hemi powerplant for factory-approved drag racing.

In 1969, the 'Cuda option took a lot of the attention away from the Barracuda S, but the model was still available with both 340 and 383 powerplants. The Formula S package again made it an enticing sports muscle machine, with a body-length stripe and heavy-duty suspension underpinnings, including a front stabilizer bar and beefy torsion bars. A small percentage of the 30,000-plus Barracudas that were sold carried this option.

Early 1970s Barracudas continued to suffer an image problem compared to the 'Cuda, which now sported both the 440 and Hemi powerplants. By 1972, the

The Formula S package presented big looks and performance for 1968. The 383 powerplant was capable of an impressive 300 horsepower, and it actually might have been more.

The '68 Barracuda was also available in notchback (shown) and convertible body styles.

biggest engine option available for the Barracuda was a downgraded 340. By 1973, the sporting aspects of the Barracuda were emphasized more than its performance. A last performance gasp — a 360-cube powerplant — was breathed in 1974, the final year for the Barracuda.

The Barracuda certainly won't be remembered in the muscle car annals to the same degree as the Road Runner, GTX, or even its companion 'Cuda, but the model provides an interesting sleeper to consider acquiring in the 1990s.

'Cuda

Little did Plymouth know what effect a Barracuda option in 1969 (Codes A56 and A57) would have on the muscle car world. These two little numbers quietly announced the start of what many consider to be the king of the vintage muscle car scene — the 'Cuda. Granted, it's a version of the Barracuda, but the 'Cuda, because of its importance in muscle car history, deserves a section of its own. It's that big.

The Code A56 package, priced at an extra $309, was the 340 engine package, while code A57 signified the 383 mill at an extra $345. Both option packages also included manual four-speed transmission, body and hood stripes, chrome-tipped dual exhausts, and heavy-duty suspension. These early 1969 models are extremely rare machines, with few positively identified today. A very limited number of 440-powered 'Cudas (about 50) were also reportedly produced that first year.

The 'Cuda really came into its own in 1970 as a distinct model in the Plymouth line. The machine came standard with a 383-cubic-inch four-barrel powerplant capable of 335 horses. Other options included the 340-cubic-inch, 275-horse engine, the six barreled 390-horse 440, the four-barreled 375-horse 440, and the king of the road, the eight-barreled 425-horse 426 Hemi — quite a power year for the 'Cuda.

The triple-carbed 440-cube, 390-horse engine was an awesome package for the 1970 'Cuda.

This magnificent 440 'Cuda belongs to Canadian Chris Coulson of Winnipeg, Manitoba. The American muscle car craze has also gone north of the border.

A flashy stripe started with a pointed arrow on the back of the front door, then swept to the rear quarter and dropped down with the engine displacement number or Hemi name contained within. It is very beneficial these days to have the Hemi lettering sitting back there, for both your spirit and your bank account! The Hemis are rare today—especially the convertibles, with only 14 built. The Hemi was a super-expensive option that added $871 to the base price. It's easy to see why there are so few around.

In all, 1970 was a very good year for the popular 'Cuda, with 16,710 hardtops and 548 convertibles built. At least partly responsible for this sales record was the 'Cuda's sporty design which included twin hood scoops, low-mounted driving lights, hood pins, and optional elastomeric front and rear bumpers. The 'Cuda was one flat-out high-performance machine in both looks and power, with 13-second quarters at 104 miles per hour.

The next year, 1971, would be the last year for the 'Cuda convertible, so if you find one, snap it up. It is known that only 17 440 Six-Barrel convertibles were built; several have already been located and restored. Even rarer are the Hemi convertibles; only 7 were built, along with a minimal run of 108 Hemi 'Cuda hardtops. In all, only 272 'Cuda convertibles and 5383 hardtops were built in 1971.

The overall appearance of the 1971 model remained very similar to the 1970 styling, although the later model did sport a vertical-ribbed grille and quad

Considered by many the most desirable of all MOPAR muscle cars, the 1970 Hemi 'Cuda, with its twin-carbed 425-horse powerplant, is bringing prices in the $100,000 range in the early 1990s.

This 1970 Hemi 'Cuda belongs to MOPAR expert Tony DePillo of Ohio.

headlights. An interesting appearance option was the billboard stripe on the rear quarter.

One year later, performance enthusiasts went into a state of shock when all the 'Cuda's big powerplants were dropped like a rock. No more 383, no more 440, and—horrors—no more Hemi! The biggest mill that could be put under a 'Cuda hood was a 340 four-barrel engine that put out a paltry 240 horses—hardly worth mentioning, considering what the 'Cuda had once been. When you really think about it, the performance era for the 'Cuda lasted for only two, or maybe three, years.

There was no doubt if your 1971 'Cuda carried the Hemi powerplant. It was the final year for the ferocious engine in the 'Cuda.

The 'Cuda still looked like a killer, but it was a façade. It still had a blacked-out hood and twin scoops, but the performance just wasn't there. In 1972, 7,628 'Cudas were sold. These models will eventually become more interesting in the collector market.

By 1973, it appeared that the 'Cuda was going the way of all the other muscle cars about this time. In 1974, the installation of a 360-cubic-inch engine that produced a barely adequate 245 ponies, didn't generate much interest; only 1191 of the 360-powered machines were sold. There's not much interest in them today, either.

It was a disappointing ending to what many consider to be the best muscle car of them all—at least in the 1969–1971 time period.

AAR 'Cuda

The 'Cuda model was covered in the previous section, but the AAR 'Cuda is a unique machine that deserves a section all its own. The flashy machine was only built for one year—1970—for an interesting reason.

The SCCA's Trans Am racing series was a great way to get a lot of exposure for a particular model, and Plymouth decided that the 'Cuda would be its entry for the series. Dan Gurney headed the team, and the AAR designation signified his All-American Racing organization. Unfortunately for Plymouth, the AAR 'Cudas were not competitive and finished far back in the final manufacturers' point standings.

There was certainly no mistaking the 1970 AAR 'Cuda. Built in limited numbers to qualify for Trans-Am racing, the AAR featured distinctive body-length stripe. Ronda Cunningham of Bloomington, Illinois, is justifiably proud of her AAR.

Granted, there were appreciable differences between the racing and street versions of the AAR, but the street version still possessed a lot of racing characteristics itself, including a rear wing and fiberglass hood. It looked like it was ready to take to the track with its outragous graphics and flashy styling.

Fans either loved the design or hated it. The street versions closely resembled the racers, with strobe racing stripes stretching the length of the body and terminating on the rear quarters with the AAR logo and medallion. Flat black was liberally used on the fender upper surfaces, grille, hood, and cowling.

Only one powerplant was available in the AAR, a 340 engine that was definitely underrated at 290 horsepower. Carrying special internal reinforcements, the 340 came in only the three-two-barrel-carb configuration. In addition, there were special heads and valve train, and an aluminum Edelbrock intake manifold. A number of racing-type suspension refinements made the AAR a real performer on both the street and strip. At least 2500 had to be built for the car to qualify for the Trans Am series, and 2724 actually made it off the line. Since many of these unique 'Cudas were used — and abused — for their intended purpose of racing, very few of them remain today.

Today, the AAR remains one of the most desirable of the 'Cudas, probably ranking second only to the top-of-the-line Hemi-powered machines. An interesting variation of the popular 'Cuda, the AAR lasted only one year, but wherever one appears, it still attracts attention. Many of the younger enthusiasts can't

The 340 Six Barrel powerplant was available only with the AAR. It was advertised at a significant 290 horsepower. By the way, the three-carb setup was not used on the real racing AARs.

believe that a company would actually produce and sell such a road-rocket to the general public. But that was business as usual at the height of the muscle car era in 1970, an era of performance that will probably never be seen again. The AAR 'Cuda certainly paints a clear picture of the way it was.

Duster

Dustin' 'em off at the dragstrip is apparently the meaning Plymouth had in mind when it introduced the sporty little Duster in 1970. Granted, it was a time when the muscle magic was disappearing, but this machine had a lot to offer and is increasing in interest for collectors in the 1990s.

Based on the lowly Valiant, the Duster provided Plymouth with the compact muscle car it needed to compete against such entries as Chevy's Nova SS. Definitely aimed toward the youth market, the Duster's 340 four-barrel power plant was capable of an advertised 275 horsepower. A somewhat radical cam and a 10.5:1 compression ratio were two reasons for the high performance. An extremely low-priced machine, the Duster 340 was a popular 1970 seller, with 24,817 constructed.

Other performance equipment on the Duster included a front stabilizer bar, large front torsion bars, special rear leaf springs and front disc brakes. The success of the Duster during its first year was no doubt the inspiration for Dodge to introduce its similar Demon the following year.

Bold graphics were the keynote for the 1971 Duster 340, the most memorable element being the optional blacked-out hood carrying a huge 340 WEDGE identification diagonally across its left front corner. Striking stripes slashed the sides of the car, and the 340 arithmetic was also displayed on the rear quarters. The horsepower figure was still 275, even a change had been made in the carburetion. The car was a low 14-second performer on the drag strip.

But the flashy new looks didn't provide much ammunition in the showroom wars; only about half as many Dusters were sold as in 1970—only 12,886 in all.

Introduced in 1970, the Plymouth Duster was a late arrival on the MOPAR muscle car scene. It was aimed at the youth market and carried a robust 340-cubic-inch engine capable of 275 horsepower.

The 1971 Duster carried a huge 340 Wedge announcement on the hood. Now that's bold.

Few of them are seen around today, but they should make excellent candidates for restoration. They can't help but appreciate in the 1990s.

The 340 powerplant began its inevitable power slide in 1972, with a net horsepower rating of 240. Even so, the Duster was still an outstanding performer at a very low price, and 15,681 buyers liked it well enough to plunk down the dollars. The $2728 base price bought a very basic Duster, but just a few appearance options could make it a tough-looking machine.

Suddenly, in 1973, performance seemed to be a bad word and the Duster body style abandoned the race-car look it carried in previous years. The 340 mill, though, was still in place and its performance was still very respectable. This would be the last year for the 340 nametag, even though 15,731 were sold.

The 340 was dead, but a new number came along for 1974, the Duster 360. Plymouth emphasized that the 360 used a lot of proven components from the previous 340, but the company didn't feel compelled to announce the numbers on the rear quarters as it had done with the 340. The 360, though, came with a number of extras, including heavy-duty suspension, disc brakes, and body striping. The Duster 360 was a disaster from a sales point of view, with just 3969 sold. This poor showroom performance was probably due to the price increase that the model required.

The Duster was a late arrival on the muscle car scene and might be around a lot longer on the muscle market of the 1990s. Although not initially as popular as its big-block-engined brothers, buyers are starting to discover the attractive little Plymouth.

GTX

When the 1967 Plymouth GTX was first introduced in late 1966, there was no doubt that this was a performance machine. It was advertised as such and it had the looks to match. A buyer could even have the monster 426 Hemi installed to make this a supercar without question, but only 125 GTXs were so-equipped that model year.

This car is one of the first GTXs, a 1967 model. It benefited greatly from the exposure it got from Richard Petty's NASCAR successes.

Tremendous exposure for that initial GTX came from the fact that NASCAR superstar Richard Petty was steering a GTX painted in his trademark blue to the championship.

The GTX came standard in 1967 with the 440-cubic-inch, 375-hp Super Commando powerplant. The suspension system matched the power with heavy-duty torsion bars and a front sway bar. With a twin-scoop hood and the long, sweeping slab sides, the GTX had a relatively successful first year, with 12,690 speeding out of the Plymouth showrooms.

In 1968, the GTX could be acquired with either of the big 426 or 440 powerplants. This beautiful example, owned by Ted Novicki of Indianapolis, carries the 426 Hemi.

The GTX's place in the spotlight lasted only one year. By 1968, its biggest competitor for performance attention and dollars was its lookalike low-budget stablemate, Plymouth's own Road Runner. Still, over 18,000 GTXs were sold in '68; 446 carried the Hemi.

The slab sides of the '69 GTX featured a body-length flat black lower panel, which, along with a slotted performance hood, made the car look like a hairy performer. An available option was the Air Grabber system that allowed cold air to be fed to the engine. Sales totaled 15,602; Hemis accounted for 986 of those.

Even though some new performance engine options were offered for the GTX in 1970, sales were poor, and just over 7,000 were built. The 440 engine was available with either a four-barrel carb or with the new Six Barrel option, which produced 390 horsepower. In order to control either the 440 or Hemi (only 72 were built) engines, the buyer got heavy-duty suspension. The 1970 GTX may be best remembered for its wide range of available colors, including bright green, orange, blue and even purple.

Emission controls were nipping at the performance of the big engines for 1971, but the GTX powerplants suffered only slight power decreases. The writing was on the wall, though, as only a minuscule 2703 were built—and this would be the GTX's last hurrah.

It should also be noted here that the standard Belvedere model, along with the similar Satellite, could also be ordered with the high-performance powerplants during this time period.

The GTX remains somewhat of a mystery car today, usually playing the role of bridesmaid to the super-popular Road Runner. Its production numbers are extremely sparse in comparison. The GTX was equipped similarly to the Road Runner, but it just never had the charisma of that Plymouth product. Investment in a GTX could prove to be a wise choice during the 1990s. They are still out there.

Road Runner

High performance and low cost were Plymouth's primary design goals for a brand-new machine in 1968. The company believed that the time was right for a factory hot rod for the young set, and its guess was right on the money.

A member of the intermediate Belvedere model line, the Road Runner came with a 383-cubic-inch engine as its standard powerplant. However, this wasn't the standard 383, as this 335-horse version used components from the 440 engine. The desirable Hemi was also an expensive ($714) option on the Runner.

Numerous other performance power train options were also available for the machine, including a specially designed four-speed and two beefed-up TorqueFlight transmissions. When the Hemi was specified, special heavy-duty suspension was also in order.

In order to keep the Road Runner's price down, Plymouth had to economize somewhere, but obviously not in the performance area. So the trim and interior had to make do with just the bare essentials.

The car's name, of course, came from the frisky little cartoon desert bird that was so popular on television at the time. The theme was carried throughout the car, with the cartoon figure appearing on the door; even the horn sounded like the Road Runner's famous "Beep-beep."

Sales of the Road Runner that first year exceeded Plymouth's most optimistic estimates to hit a total of 44,599. The overwhelming majority of the Runners were equipped with the standard 383, but just over 1,000 came through with the awesome 426 Hemi, making this the most common Hemi car ever produced. A number of those Hemi Road Runners are still around and they are fetching fantastic money. (A word to the wise: Check that that Hemi originally sat in that engine compartment and wasn't installed later for monetary gain.) But even the 383 cars are attractive, too, from both performance and investment standpoints.

Plymouth knew it had a good thing going with the Road Runner and made it even better for 1969. A key addition to the engine compartment was an optional Air Grabber induction system. A solid ductwork connection was made between the hood scoops and engine once the hood was closed. Coyote Duster was the catchy name given to the system, a decal of which was attached to the air cleaner on the 383 power plant.

Being named *Motor Trend*'s Car of the Year for 1969 certainly didn't hurt the Road Runner's sales, as 84,420 of the speedy models were sold. As in 1968, most of the cars were powered with the 383 engine, but there were still a few of the Hemi machines built — 788 to be exact. The 440 Six-Barrel, complete with a flat black all-fiberglass lift-off hood, was also a popular powerplant option. Originally designed on a low-cost post coupe body, the Runner proved so popular that a convertible was added for 1969 (a hardtop had joined the fleet in mid-1968).

The standard 383 powerplant experienced a slight decrease in compression ratio for 1970, but surprisingly no drop in its 335 horsepower figure. Everything else remained about the same as the era of the Plymouth rapid-transit system was in high gear.

In addition to the Hemi engine, the three-Holley carb-equipped-440 engine

The Road Runner was a real winner for 1969, as it was named the *Motor Trend* Car of the Year. The 383-cubic-incher was the standard powerplant.

The Hemi was available in the Road Runner through the 1971 model.

was also available. This produced a ground-pounding 390 horsepower and cost the buyer an extra $250 over the 383's base price. The sides of the pop-up Air Grabber door were eye-catching if you happened to be alongside to do street battle. Etched on the sides were evil-looking shark's teeth.

Sales of the 1970 Road Runners dropped substantially, down to 43,404. Like Road Runners of the previous years, the 1970 models remain highly collectible.

A sizable drop in compression ratio for 1971 cut the heart out of the 383 engine, dropping the horsepower value down to just 300. A slight compression drop didn't hurt the announced characteristics of the Hemi, but five horses did melt away from the 440 engine.

A nice appearance option for the all-new 1971 Road Runner was the introduction of a rear deck spoiler. But sales dropped even faster than the compression ratio, with just 14,484 sold. The Road Runner's companion, the GTX, had such a poor sales showing that year that the model was ended. The Road Runner was more fortunate.

The sales trend continued downward in 1972 with just 7,628 Runners sold. Their attractiveness as muscle collectibles today is also considerably less than the late 1960s models. The 383 engine was replaced in number only as it was bored out to 400 inches; power was a very modest 255 net. A four-barrel version of the 440 was also available and capable of 280 horses.

For all practical purposes, the muscle era was over for the Road Runner when it carried the 318 engine as the standard power plant for 1973. Choked-

The 1969 introduced Six Pack version of the 440. Lower hp versions of the 440 were available in the Road Runner through 1974.

down versions of the 340, 400, and 440 engines were still available, and a 360-cubic-inch mill couldn't rekindle the fire in 1974.

To many, the Road Runner of the late 1960s and early 1970s epitomizes the best of the vintage muscle machines. With its stripped-down body and powerful engines, the Road Runner was fast, real fast, and its values in the 1990s will continue to hold it at a high level.

Three of the best Road Runners. Gathered are examples of the 1968, 1970, and 1971 models.

THE WINGED WONDERS: DODGE DAYTONA AND PLYMOUTH SUPERBIRD

Now we're really talking wild and crazy, completely unbelievable, with looks like a rocket ship. The Dodge Daytona, built only in 1969, and the Plymouth Superbird of 1970 looked like they were capable of challenging the Saturn V for its first manned trip to the moon.

These winged wonders were built for one purpose and one purpose only—NASCAR racing. They definitely had what it took with Hemi power and unbelievable aerodynamics. To prove the capability, NASCAR driver Buddy Baker toured the Talladega Speedway high banks at over 200 miles per hour for the first time. Several drivers have stated that these cars, with modern tires, could still compete with the modern stockers. Let's look at each machine separately, the Daytona first.

The prototype of the Daytona actually started with the body of a Dodge Charger. But when the Dodge engineers got done with it, it sure didn't bear much resemblance to the standard version. At the front was a swoopy nosepiece that added 19 inches, stretching the car's overall length to 221 inches. Built by Creative Industries, the nosepiece carried a short spoiler underneath and pop-up headlight doors. The addition reportedly added 200 pounds of downforce at speed.

But the nose was only half of the Daytona's body design innovations. At the other end, a 25-inch-high wing cut the wind to create hundreds of pounds of downforce. Owners of these cars in the 1990s say that the aerodynamics really work, and that the effects can be felt at about 60 or 70 miles per hour. Imagine what it must have felt like at 200 miles per hour!

Either the 440 or 426 Hemi powerplants were the engine choices. As if it really needed to be announced, the Daytona name screamed at you from the rear quarters. The lettering was the car's base color outlined by the stripe color, which streaked vertically up the rear fender and across the fiberglass rear wing. Two transmissions were available on the Daytona, heavy-duty versions of the

Dave Jones of Indianapolis is the lucky owner of both this 1969 Dodge Daytona and a 1970 Plymouth Superbird. The pair of winged models are two of the most desirable of the MOPAR muscle machines, built in limited numbers to qualify for NASCAR racing.

Dave Jones's 1970 Superbird.

manual four-speed and the three-speed Torqueflite. All this performance was required, though, since the Daytona grossed out at about two tons.

Daytona performance was impressive, with 0 to 60 in about 7 seconds and the quarter-mile in the 13-second category. But surprisingly, only 503 of the Daytonas were produced, just enough to qualify the car for NASCAR racing. And, quite frankly, the Daytona just didn't catch the public's fancy as Dodge had figured. Since Daytonas (and the later Plymouth Superbirds) sat on car lots for many months. Some dealers reportedly had to convert the winged wonders back into standard models in order to get them sold.

The Daytona showed that it really had the stuff on the superspeedways, causing Plymouth to reconsider building its own version. Superbird was the name selected, and Plymouth made a number of changes on its design, based on Dodge's experiences with the Daytona.

Differences included a smaller front spoiler on the nose and a lower location for the cooling vent. The redesign of the rear wing resulted in a taller and more swept-back shape and made it much more efficient. The extremely successful Road Runner served as the starting point for the Superbird. Plymouth hoped that car's success would cascade down on the new creation. New NASCAR rules required an additional number of cars (one per dealer) be built in 1970, resulting in a Superbird production run of 1903.

The graphics of the Superbird were completely different from the Daytona, and there is little chance of ever confusing the two, even though the external bodies appeared almost identical. Huge Plymouth scripting almost completely covered the rear quarters, while a circled Road Runner emblem was carried externally on each wing mount and on the left pop-up headlight door.

The cars certainly got their share of publicity, with Richard Petty and Pete Hamilton bringing their Superbirds home to eight victories. But NASCAR didn't like that kind of domination, and for the 1971 season the cars were slapped with engine power reductions in the form of carburetor restrictor plates that reduced the mixture flow. (The same technique was brought back to life by NASCAR in the late 1980s to slow the cars again.)

The final season for the NASCAR Superbirds and Daytonas was 1971. That year would also end one of the most interesting production programs of the musclecar era.

With so few of the winged cars built, it's amazing how many of them are still around. They are hard to miss at a muscle car meet. Just gaze over a field of machines and the distinctive Daytona and Superbird wings shoot to the sky.

These models have to rate as two of the most coveted muscle cars, with prices in the high five figures not uncommon in the 1990s. If you have never before seen one of these magnificent streamliners, you would swear that the technology looks more like the 1990s than the late 1960s. Imagine what these cars might have become if they had been allowed to evolve over the years.

CHAPTER V

American Motors Muscle Cars

WHEN YOU ARE NUMBER FOUR (OF FOUR), YOU HAVE TO TRY HARDER. THAT'S exactly the situation tiny American Motors Corporation found itself in when the Big Three started getting into the muscle car game in the mid-1960s.

AMC, however, got a late start and the going was tough against the established muscle makers. It took a long time for AMC to start building the required bigger engines, their first effort being a somewhat anemic 290-cubic-inch powerplant in 1966. The advertised horsepower was only 225. Compared to the competition of the time—the Chrysler Hemis, the 390 Ford Fairlanes, the SS396 Chevelles, and the 389 Tri-Power GTOs—it left a lot to be desired from a performance point of view.

Later in the decade, the company would continue to play catch-up with 343-, 360-, 390-, and 401-cubic-inch engines. It seemed, though, that the AMC muscle machines got more attention from their appearance than from their performance. A number of the models used wild but patriotic color schemes; the SC/Rambler, Hurst Super Stock AMX, and Rebel Machine models all came through in red, white, and blue paint jobs. There has never been anything like them since.

AMC looked to racing to aid in merchandising its products. The company contracted with Roger Penske to run its Javelins in the Trans Am series and came away with a championship. In fact, one of the Trans Am drivers, Mark Donohue, had a special Javelin model named in his honor.

AMX

The change from its econobox image to the flashy and stylish AMX was a leap of monumental proportions for AMC. The design, though, was basically a major modification of the existing Javelin, which was shortened about a foot and then stuffed with a potent 390 engine along with sports-type suspension and other performance add-ons. The first of the models, known as the AMX 390, were introduced at the 1968 Daytona Speed Weeks and people liked what they saw.

AMX stood for American Motors Experimental and represented the first all-metal two-seat American sports car in a dozen years; 6725 were sold that first (1968) model year. The sales figure increased to 8293 in the second of its three years and quietly closed out at only 4116 the final year.

A 290-cubic-inch, 225 horsepower AMC engine was the base powerplant for the AMX in the 1968 and 1969 model years. The optional Go Package consisted of the more potent 343- or 390-cubic-inch engines, 70-series tires, twin-grip rear end, front disc brakes, twin racing stripes, and lots of additional heavy-duty equipment. The AMX stickered for $3245 with an extra $310 needed for the Go Package performance goodies.

It sounds potent, and it was. In fact, Craig Breedlove used a specially equipped AMX in February of 1968 to establish 106 world records at the Goodyear test facility.

Because of its late introduction the previous year, few changes were made to the '69 AMX. The same engine options were available, but a new 140-mile-per-hour speedometer and larger tach enticed those who dared. A special 1969 model run was named the Big Bad AMX. The model was available in only three colors—bright orange, blue, and green—and had the bumpers painted the same color as the sheetmetal; 742 were produced and today are in great demand among those addicted to the AMC label.

Considerable facelifting and performance changes were made in the AMX for 1970. A completely restyled front end, a functional cold-air ram induction hood, a slight reduction in height, and a two-inch increase in length gave the AMX the look of a real racing machine. The standard powerplant was a 360-

The AMX was built from 1968 through 1970. This model is a 1969.

The AMX received a new grille and other minor changes for its final year, 1970.

cubic-inch, 290-horse mill hooked up with dual exhausts. As before, the Go Package was also available on these, the last of the AMXs.

An interesting footnote to the story are the 52 white 1969 AMXs that were modified by Hurst for Super Stock drag racing. These machines carried specially modified 390-cubic-inch, 340-horse powerplants, heavy-duty axles, special suspension, and a ton of other dragstrip necessities. The machines were obviously built to run and were sold mostly to dealers and race teams. An unknown

The 390-cubic-inch powerplant was top AMC muscle for 1968 through 1970.

number were delivered in AMC's special red, white, and blue graphic paint scheme. Fewer than half of the 52 cars have been discovered, and they are extremely valuable collectibles.

Javelin

The unsuccessful Marlin model (a sporty fastback roof grafted onto a standard sedan, with no guts whatsoever) was the forerunner of the Javelin, AMCs entry into the pony car race, which appeared in 1968. The Javelin SST was the sporty model, with reclining bucket seats and special trim options. AMC 343- and 290-cubic-inch powerplants were available in any Javelin. Weighing in at slightly over 3100 pounds, the Javelin was one snappy performance machine. A good showing of 55,124 sold that first year was cause for enthusiasm from the AMC brass.

Only minor trim changes were made to the Javelin for 1969, but there were a number of special models during the year; 343 and 390 Go Package options were also available.

Special models also abounded in 1970, including the Javelin SST, which carried a floor-mounted three-speed shifter and other appearance options. Additionally, two limited production versions of the SST were the Javelin SST Trans Am (of which only 100 were produced) and 2501 of the Mark Donohue special autograph versions. The production numbers enabled the machines to run on the SCCA Trans Am circuit.

For 1971, AMC completely reshaped the Javelin with race-car body aerodynamics. Many of the new design innovations were the result of work done by

1970 was the last year for the original Javelin body introduced in 1968. This one's an SST powered by a snappy 360.

American Motor's biggest engine, a 401, could be had in the 1971 through 1974 model years of the Javelin AMX.

Penske and Donohue on the innovative design. The interior had an aircraft look about it. The three versions available—Javelin, Javelin SST and Javelin/AMX— were trimmed out to increasing levels; 29,130 Javelins of all types were produced. Again, the Go Package was available for the AMX version with both the 360- and the new 401-cubic-inch power plants.

Only minimal changes were made to the line for 1972, but the base Javelin line was dropped in favor of SST and AMX versions. An interesting addition to

The Javelin AMX, one sharp sports machine, could be acquired with the powerful 401-cubic-inch powerplant. Here, a 401-powered 1973 model shows its lines.

the line was the Javelin/Pierre Cardin option, which featured a luxurious interior and Cardin crests mounted on the exterior sheetmetal.

The Javelin stayed pretty much the same for 1973 even though the nation's love affair with the muscle car was on a downward trend. For 1974—the car's final year—a substantial design change took place. Production estimates vary according to source, but it appears that approximately 28,000 Javelins were produced with 4980 AMX models. It was a strong finish for an interesting muscle machine.

Hurst SC/Rambler

If you're old enough, you can probably still remember the little American Motors car known as the Rambler American. A square, underpowered vehicle, the car was exactly what the little old lady next door might drive to the grocery store and church. But in 1969, AMC produced a version of the little econobox that would have made that old lady's hair stand on end. Without a doubt, the Hurst-modified SC/Rambler caught everyone's attention in a big way.

There was plenty of punch under the SC/Rambler's hood, with a 390-cubic-inch, 315-horse V-8 capable of punching out 425 foot-pounds of torque. The transmission was a close-ratio Borg-Warner four-speed; the suspension system was high-tech with an independent link system up front and a five-leaf semi-elliptical leaf arrangement in place of the rear. The company advertised the SC (which was classified as a 1969½ model) to be a spirited performer and showed the figures to back it up. The SC was definitely a 14-second car in the 100-mile-per-hour range—very competitive performance for the time period.

Chris Blue of Springfield, Ohio, owns this flashy Hurst SC/Rambler powered by a potent 390-cubic-inch, 315-horsepower engine. The SC/Rambler was a one-year (1969) muscle machine produced in two distinctly different color schemes.

But it was the patriotic graphic styling that really made this machine an eye-catcher. The A-Type color scheme featured a white base coat, a body-length red side slab, and a wide blue racing stripe tailing over the complete length of the center body. The interesting aspect of the design was a large blue arrow on the hood pointing toward a huge, protruding hood scoop and the lettering 390 Cubic Inches. There was no mistaking an SC when you saw one; the car really had the look of a hot-rod street machine.

Initially, American Motors planned on producing a run of only 500, but the company quickly realized that estimate was going to be far short of demand; 1512 were eventually built. Interestingly, not all of the SCs were built with the initial wild paint scheme. A number of them came through with a calmer B-Type design, which was mostly white punctuated with red and blue striping. These B vehicles had the same power train options, but are considered extremely rare on today's muscle car market.

The SC/Rambler was a case of starting too late in the muscle car fight for customers. The Rambler name also probably hurt the gutsy little machine, but with the SC/Rambler and the earlier AMXs, the company definitely proved it was capable. If AMC had begun development in the mid-1960s, the results might have been different.

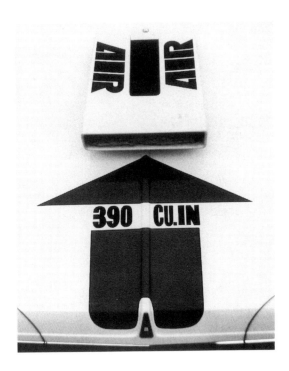

When staid AMC decided to get in the muscle game with the 1969 Hurst SC/Rambler, it wasn't bashful about letting the world know. This is not the hood of some customized hot rod—it's the SC/Rambler's A-type scheme right off the showroom floor.

REBEL MACHINE

This 1970 AMC muscle effort was also painted red, white, and blue, had a high-performance powerplant, and would be just a one-year offering with only 1900 produced.

Using a basic white base coat, the Rebel Machine featured a blue hood including the scoop and a red side stripe that widened as it ran high on the length of the body. The stripe terminated in a red, white, and blue band across the rear deck. It also sported a blacked-out hood and fender tops.

Like the SC/Rambler, the Rebel Machine also carried patriotic colors. Available only in 1970, the Machine toted a 340-horse version of the 390 cubic-inch-powerplant. This one's owned by Rick Riley of Middletown, Ohio.

Although the Rebel Machine weighed in at a healthy 3650 pounds, its 390 powerplant was up to the job of getting it down the road. Instead of the 315-horsepower version that came in the SC/Rambler, a 340-horse version was available in the Machine. The package featured a functional vacuum-operated hood scoop and hood-mounted 8000-rpm tachometer. The Borg-Warner T-10 four-speed (or an automatic flood shift) and a wide variety of rear-end ratios made the Rebel Machine a solid 14-second performer on the drag strip. As with the SC/Rambler, Hurst performance was also involved in modifying the Machine.

CHAPTER VI

Factory Racing Muscle Cars

THE 1960S WAS A DECADE WHEN THE BIG THREE CAR COMPANIES WENT RACING in a big way. Their activity covered all realms of the racing environment—drag, road course, and oval. In fact, there is a good chance that a number of the most famous of the street muscle cars would never have appeared had it not been for racing.

Cars such as the AAR 'Cuda, Firebird Trans Am, and Z/28 all had racing roots. The specially built racing machines were also heavily used in advertising the street versions of the cars. Many of these racers have been found and restored, and today their values can reach into the six-figure range for some models. They are highly coveted among muscle collectors, and the interest and nostalgia of the old racers grows yearly. Their numbers are, of course, very few, but they are certainly some of the most important of all muscle machines.

DRAG CARS

Let's first check out the drag versions of these cars and look at a few that remain. It should be noted that many of these cars were raced for many years and received numerous modifications through their lives. Many lost their identity completely; others, through extensive research, have been identified and restored. These magnificent recollections of drag muscle past recall a factory involvement that will probably never return. There were more factory drag machines than are discussed here—a lot more—but these should be enough to whet your appetite.

The unlikely Ford Falcon was the recipient of factory drag reworking in 1964 and 1965. Called the A/FX (Factory Experimental) Falcon 427, only two actually were sponsored by the Ford factory. The A/FX was an awesome drag machine, with the 427 engine kicking out an estimated 550 horsepower. The car

Comet Cyclone is one of the rare A/FX factory race Comets.

also came with a four-speed and a Detroit Locker 31-spline rear end. It was reportedly capable of over 120 miles per hour in the quarter mile. John Gotshall of Canton, Ohio, has one of the rare machines, and he still blows it out down the strip once in awhile.

For the counterpart Mercury factory dragster, the names were A/FX and B/FX. The A version carried the 427 powerplant, while the B model had the small-block 289 mill. Like the Falcon A/FXs, these modified Comets were assembled at the Stroppe Racing Shop in California. The cars were not street-legal and were never offered to the public for sale. They stickered for only $3800 and certainly weren't noted for their comfort.

The Comets and Falcons were sent to Stroppe from the factory without doors, dashes, front fenders, hoods, bumpers, or sound-deadening material. Most of the deleted parts were replaced with fiberglass components to make the cars super-light.

One of the most famous of the A/FX Comets was The Wedge King, which

The Number 647 A/FX was the winner of the 1965 Winternationals. This rare Comet has been completely restored.

won the 1965 Winternationals. It had a best quarter-mile time of 10.5 seconds. The number 647 car is still with us, has been completely restored, and now makes exhibition runs. It's still got it!

Wayne Conover of Hanover, Pennsylvania, owns one of the rare B/FX cars—and rare is definitely the correct description of this machine. Conover says that only a half-dozen of the cars remain today.

Even the Ford Galaxie, that luxury full-size car, was also a part of the drag scene. A lightweight version of the car was available in the mid-1960s; 211 were produced in 1963. The first 20 became the factory racers and the rest were sold to the buying public. These cars have aluminum bumpers and brackets along with fiberglass front ends, hoods, fenders, deck lid, and doors. Power for these muscular Galaxies came from a hulking 427-cubic-inch, 425-horse Ford Wedge powerplant hooked up to an aluminum Borg-Warner transmission with a 2.36 first gear ratio. Skip Norman owns one of the cars and he still runs the nearly 30-year-old machine. He's turned 11.55 seconds at 120 mph in the quarter.

Then there was the Ford Thunderbolt. The name said it all. This machine was every bit a bolt of thunder with an 11-second quarter-mile capability right out of the box.

With the power of advertising being such a factor in those years, several Ford dealers had modified earlier Fairlanes into drag machines. It wasn't until 1963, though, that a factory effort was undertaken along those lines. Exactly how many of these factory rocket Thunderbolts were built is still being argued, but suffice it to say that the number was around 100.

The T-bolts looked deceptively stock from the outside—except for the bulge in the fiberglass hood, which was needed to cover the crammed-in 427 powerplant that produced something in the neighborhood of 500 horses. A certain amount of engine compartment modification was also necessary to accomplish the conversion.

The T-bolt was not a muscle car to drive on the street. When fired up, the engine exploded with power and decibels. Toting 12.7:1 forged aluminum pistons, a forged steel crank, twin carbs, and a high-lift cam, the motor provided brutal acceleration. The remainder of the power train included a highly modified C-6 transmission and a Detroit Locker rear end.

Ford got in the factory drag-racing game early, as evidenced by this 1963 Super/Stock Galaxie.

Only about 100 of these 1964 Ford Thunderbolt factory drag machines were built. Everything about them spelled performance, and it was all done under factory auspices. The cars are practically priceless in the early 1990s.

Mention Thunderbolt to a Ford muscle fanatic and you'll see eyeballs bulge. These are legitimate six-figure cars, and at such prices, the buyer should be sure he's getting the real item and not a decked-out Fairlane. Again—and we'll keep repeating it—let the buyer beware.

A number of early Mustangs were also converted into factory drag machines. Brent and Terrie Hajek own a number of these factory racers, including the Mustang once driven by drag-racing legend Gas Ronda. Ronda drove the now-restored car in both 1966 and 1967, and it was capable of turning eights in its day.

A famous factory racer, this Mustang drag car was driven by Gas Ronda. It's one of a fleet of former factory racers owned by Brent and Terrie Hajek, who put on exhibitions with the cars.

The car carried a 427 SOHC powerplant and a C-6 transmission. The bright orange racer now makes many exhibition runs across the nation, reviving a lot of old drag-racing memories.

The Mr. 4-Speed was a 1965 factory A/FX Mustang campaigned by Wickersham Ford that made it to the 1965 AHRA finals. It was one of only 10 built and has been completely restored.

A few of the potent Shelby Mustangs were also converted into factory drag racers. In 1965 and 1966, there were nine and four GT-350s, respectively, modified for that use.

In another interesting performance experiment, Ford assembled 54 428-cubic-inch-powered Mustang Cobra Jets for dealer drag activities. The first four cars were driven by a number of the then-heavyweights of the sport, while the rest went to any dealer who had the bucks and the desire to race. John Lambing of Hamilton, Ohio, now has one of these rare machines, and he's completely traced the history of the car back to its beginning at Frontier Ford of Niagara Falls, New York.

Lambing also owns a rare Boss 429 Mustang equipped with a special S-engined version of the potent powerplant. The special engine had stronger internal components for durability. With a 10.5:1 compression ratio and 730 CFM Holley Carb, these cars were great campaigners. Lambing's particular car started its career at an Iowa Ford dealer.

Gary Hortonoff of North Canton, Ohio, is the owner of a rare 1970 Pro Stock Mustang factory racer. The car was campaigned for one year with driver Dave Lyall at the wheel. The present owner has restored it to brand-new condition. It's an awesome performer, with the correct 429 Boss topped by two 660 Holley

This factory A/FX Mustang was one of only ten built. This restored machine was originally campaigned by Wickersham Ford of Orange, Texas.

This Boss 429 K-engined Mustang is owned by John Lambing, who demonstrated on his own driveway that the car's still got it!

carbs. The engine was a milestone powerplant, as it carried the first Wiand Tunnel Ram for the Boss motor. Horsepower was reportedly in the 700 range.

Moving into the Bowtie line, some very rare lightweight Chevy factory dragsters were built. Production numbers of these cars are unattainable, but certainly very low. The Zintsmaster-sponsored 1962 lightweight Impala Super Sport illustrated is a prime example of those cars, which terrorized the strips during the early 1960s with their potent 409s. The model came from the factory, sans radio and heater, with metallic brakes, 4.56 axle, factory tach, bucket seats, four-speed transmission, and finally, the twin-carbed version of the immortal 409. It's been restored back to its former glory.

Other factory drag racers are certainly still out there racing without their owners even knowing what valuable machines they are. Others will be found in the future, but not many are left. Look carefully for these very valuable factory drag machines. They're worth the hunt.

This 1962 lightweight Impala Super Sport was sponsored by Zintsmaster Chevrolet and carries the twin-carbed 409 powerplant under the hood. Almost completely original, the vintage machine is priceless to muscle drag fans.

ROAD RACERS

The SCCA Trans Am road course series was a great motivator for the building of muscle cars in the 1960s. In fact, the series was directly responsible for the T/A Challenger, AAR 'Cuda, Z/28 Camaro, Boss 302 Mustang, and others.

The looks of these machines were definitely race-oriented, and those looks hold great value today on the auction floor. The street versions of these Trans Am cars are one thing, but finding an example of one of the real race cars is a muscle prize of the first order.

Ford's Shelby Mustangs were early participants, with 37 built in 1965, 16 notchback models built in 1966, 26 in 1967, and seven in 1967. A few of these rare muscle racers have been identified.

Jon Carey of Auburnville, Massachusetts, owns one of the '65 racers, but it's not just any Mustang—it's the very same car that was campaigned by the young Mark Donohue. It's an amazing machine that looks very much like its other GT-350 brothers, with white body and blue striping.

Low weight was an important racing requirement; hence this machine carries no bumpers, heater, headliner, carpeting, glovebox, or trunk lock. Inside, there's a factory roll bar, racing bucket seat, and everything else you would expect in a road-racing machine. Power comes from a potent 289-cubic-inch, 375-horse engine, which kicked out 340 pounds of torque at 4200 rpm.

The most famous of the Ford Trans Am racers, though, were the Boss 302 machines. There was a world of difference between the racer and the street

The Number 78 Shelby was once the mount of Mark Donohue; the early GT 350 carries a 289-cubic-inch, 375-horse powerplant.

The Boss 302 Mustang was an avid Trans Am performer. This prototype version is owned by David Tom of Cincinnati, Ohio.

version. The 302 racing powerplant was listed at 460 horses, compared to only 290 for the street version.

The Bosses were dominant on the racetrack, with Parnelli Jones, Peter Revson, and George Follmer blowing away the competition in 1970. A number

The famous Penske/Donohue 1967 Camaro, painted Sunoco Blue, was powered by a 304-cubic-inch, 402-horsepower engine.

Roger Penske would also build a Trans Am racer with AMC backing. That vehicle was based on a 1970 Javelin and kicked out 450 willing ponies from its 304 cubes. Needless to say, these vintage racers have reached astronomical values.

of these cars have been found and restored, and some are still raced today at vintage meets. The values of these cars—especially those with documented racing pasts—are unbelievable.

Talk about Trans Am racing and it's impossible not to mention the name of the incomparable Roger Penske. Based on Camaro Z/28s, the Penske machines were outstanding performers in the late 1960s. The Sunoco Blue Chevies were powered by 304-cubic-inch engines with horsepower ratings in excess of 400. The 3050-pound racers could also get down the dragstrip, with 12.7-second, 115-mph quarter-mile clockings. Their top speed was in the 140-mph range. Like the Boss 302 cars, the restored Penske/Donohue Camaros are worth a king's ransom today.

It should be noted that a number of Boss Mustangs and Camaros ran with smaller teams. These too are valuable machines, but certainly not as valuable as the cars of the famous teams.

Even AMC got into the act, with Roger Penske taking a foundering team and, Mark Donohue and Peter Revson at the wheel, bringing home a championship. Brooke Musgrave of Columbus, Ohio, found one of the old Penske T/A Javelins and accomplished an unbelievable restoration.

The car was powered by an AMC 304-cubic-inch mill, which kicked out a healthy 450 horses at 7500 rpm. Musgrave's magnificent restoration is regularly raced on the vintage circuit.

Their numbers are small, but the desirability of these old Trans Am cars is high. They are an important part of the musclecar scene, having been instrumental in the design of a number of street versions of the cars. Acquiring one and restoring it in its original livery would make a great racing machine and an outstanding investment.

CHAPTER VII

Indy Pace Cars

THAT MAGIC EVENT THAT OCCURS EVERY MEMORIAL DAY WEEKEND, THE INDY 500, has a mystique about it that is unmatched. The national exposure is unbelievable, a situation that has not been overlooked by the car companies through the years. Each year, one manufacturer has the honor of providing the Indy 500's official pace car. Every time the great race has been run, it has been led by a pace car, but only in recent years have the manufacturers realized the advantages of that honor for advertising purposes.

The actual pace cars (the two or three that do the pacing of the race) are usually modified to reach the speed required for pacing duties. In most cases, the actual pace cars get a hopped-up engine and special suspensions.

In addition to the actual pacers, though, a number of replica pace cars are produced during the model year. These replicas usually fall into the musclecar category, and their collectibility is increasing steadily.

The years 1964 through 1972 were extremely exciting ones for pace car fans, with all three of the major car builders represented. General Motors paced the race in four of those years, with Camaro in 1967 and 1969 and Oldsmobile in 1970 and 1972. Ford was represented with the '64 Mustang, the '66 Mercury, and the '68 Torino. Chrysler showed its colors with a Plymouth Sport Fury in 1965 and a bright orange Dodge Challenger in 1971.

Many of these replicas were delivered to the showroom without the identifying Indy decals. In other cases, the buyers requested that the flashy logos be removed before the purchase. Many of these interesting muscle cars have thus lost their identities through the years with modifications and repaintings. Knowledgable collectors, though, in some cases have been able to identify replicas through research and restore them back to their Indy trim. Many of the replicas carry the desirable big-block engines, making them even more valuable. But, as is the case with so many other types of muscle cars in the 1990s, the temptation to fake a pace car is great.

GENERAL MOTORS PACE CARS

Two of the GM cars selected during this time span were full-sized sedans, while the other two were sport models. Oldsmobile bowed in with a pair of dashing 4-4-2 machines. The actual 1970 pacers carried 455-cubic-inch, 365-horsepower blueprinted W-30 powerplants hooked to fully synchronized three-speed heavy-duty manual transmissions and Hurst shifters. The Olds pacers also carried heavy-duty suspension features, such as front and rear stabilizer bars.

The 1970 4-4-2 pacers and their replicas carried black and red striping and black interior trim. Some 626 replicas were produced, 358 of them Cutlass S convertibles with the 350 power plant; 269 4-4-2s with the 455. The latter big-block cars are, of course, the most sought-after and the most valuable.

Even though the Olds '72 replicas didn't carry the performance package of the real pacers, they are still attractive muscle machines. With the 4-4-2 replica, the W-30 powerplant was the high-performance engine option. Other normal power train components included the Turbo-Hydramatic with a Hurst Dual-Gate shifter and a 3.23 rear axle. Every Hurst also came with Rallye suspension, powe front disc brakes, and dual exhausts. We're talking one very classy muscle pacer here!

Now, let's move back a few years to the well-known Camaro pace cars of 1967 and 1969. All of the Camaro pace cars carried both the SS and RS option packages. Engine choices were the 350 and 396 powerplants with either four-speed or automatic transmissions.

Very few (probably about a hundred) of the '67 cars were built. Three pace cars were specially modified for the actual race. The 396 engines for these on-track pace cars were blueprinted and the chassis components were magna-fluxed. Also, special engine drivebelts, along with high-capacity alternators and radiators, were installed.

The popularity of the '67 pacer inspired Chevy to produce 3675 streetable pace car replicas for the '69 version. There were great appearance similarities

A restored 1970 Olds 4-4-2 pace car replica. A second replica sits beside it.

A Camaro SS/RS paced the 1967 Indy 500.

between the two years, with the most noticable difference being the change from blue interior and trim on with '67 to a bright orange for 1969.

The on-track pace cars for 1969, just as two years earlier, were modified for their official duties. Again, a specially prepared 396 big-block served as the powerplant, hooked up to a Turbo 400 transmission and a 12-bolt Positraction rear end. Disc brakes were in place on all four corners.

The '69 Camaro replicas used both 350 and 396 powerplants and externally were identical to the on-track machines. Orange striping was in place over the Dover White paint, along with white body sills and rear panel. The '69 Camaro is one of the most popular of the pace cars on the current musclecar market, and it's been said that of the 3675 built, some 5000 remain. Again, buyer beware!

Probably the best-known pace car of all time is the 1969 Camaro SS/RS. There seem to be more of these around today than Chevrolet actually built in 1969 — and they built 3675.

FORD PACE CARS

Ford participated heavily in the pace car competition during this time period. Following the use of a Thunderbird in the 1961 race, the Ford label was in place three more times during the 1960s — Mustang in 1964, Comet in 1966, and Torino in 1968.

The Mustang was probably the most popular pace car ever. Its selection also marked the shortest time between model introduction and naming as the pace car — only two weeks.

Externally, the Mustang pacers looked completely stock, with the exception of the Indy lettering that graced their sides. The two actual pace cars carried 289 Hi-Po powerplants along with Borg-Warner T-10 four-speed transmissions. Their suspension systems were given special attention to handle the high-speed turns during the pacing of the race.

In addition to the convertibles that were built for duties at the track, Ford also scheduled production of 185 identically prepared replicas with 260-cubic-inch powerplants, automatic transmissions and 3.00 rear axles. A number of these pacers have been located and restored — very few, though.

The winner of the big race in 1964 was A.J. Foyt. As is the custom, he was given one of the real pace cars as part of his victory loot. He gave the car to his maid, and it was well-used. The car has never been located after it was sold.

Two years later, Mercury Division made the most of the selection of its Comet as the leader of the race. The model was also touted by one publication as the "Performance Car of the Year." Deviating from the normal white Indy pacer color scheme, Mercury painted the cars that year in a dazzling candy-apple red with white racing stripes. Large white lettering on the cars' flanks and a small checkered flag on the front fenders were the identifiers for the model.

The Comet pacer was advertised as carrying the 335-horsepower version of Ford's 390-cubic-inch mill. The real pacers had the expected suspension modifications, but little is known about the number of replicas constructed. Only a very few have been located.

Ford built three actual Torino pace cars for the 1968 race, equipping them with 428 Cobra Jet powerplants and other modifications. What happened to

The Mercury Cornet GT was the 1966 Indy pace car.

Everybody knows about the '67 and '69 Camaros, but how many remember that a Ford Torino set the Indy pace in 1968?

those cars is unknown. The replicas carried the 302-cubic-inch engine, although it is rumored that the car could be ordered with a larger powerplant.

CHRYSLER PACE CARS

Bookended by two Ford pace car years, Chrysler had the honor in 1965 with a Hemi-powered Sport Fury convertible. A total of 6272 Sport Fury convertibles were constructed that model year, but how many of them were converted into pace car replicas is unknown.

A number of the Fury pacers have been located. Solid identification can be made on this model, since Plymouth placed a dash plate on each car with the words "Official Pace Car, Indianapolis 500 Race 1965."

Six years later, Chrysler showed up again at the Brickyard, but it occurred under strange circumstances. For the first time, in 1971, the factories were not

The 1971 Indy pacer was the Dodge Challenger. Since Indianapolis-area dealers, rather than the factory, put these cars together, a lot of variation is evident among the official replicas.

officially involved with the pace-car project. The Dodge Challenger pace car was the private undertaking of a number of local Indianapolis Dodge dealers, and the actual pace car was driven by one of the dealers, Eldon Palmer. Unfortunately, Palmer crashed the car along pit lane when he hit a photographers' stand.

Following the race, the remaining Challengers were distributed among the Indy Dodge dealers and sold to the public. There are indications that other Dodge dealers around the country ordered the orange convertibles with a number of different options and installed the pace car decals. The 50 pace-car replicas that were at the track had some common traits, including flat hoods and white tops and interior; a majority of them were probably equipped with the potent 383 powerplant. Other replicas have been identified with the 340 engine. Even though there was no corporate involvement with these cars, the 1971 Challenger was one of the best-looking of all the pacers.

They are a strange breed, these pace-car muscle machines. But they are muscle cars in every sense of the definition. Add the aura of Indy to these machines and you have a muscle car with a little extra pizzazz, which will bring big money in the coming years.

CHAPTER VIII

Muscle Car Restoration

SO YOU'D LOVE TO OWN A BIG BLOCK MUSCLE CAR THAT HAS ALL THE options. Who wouldn't?

You have two alternatives. The first is to lay down big bucks for an authentic, completely-restored car. The rarer the model and the better the restoration, the higher the cost will be. Make sure, of course, when putting down those big dollars, that what you are getting is what you *think* you are getting.

The second way to acquire your dream machine is a lot more economical — and a lot more risky. It involves buying a car in need of restoration. Restoration can mean anything from a little detailing to a complete rebuilding of the car.

WHAT IS RESTORATION?

To restore a car to the standards now in place for the 1990s means a lot more than it did earlier. Today's standards have reached a seemingly ridiculous level. Everything has to be exactly the way it was when the car was manufactured, even down to flaws and oversprays during the building process. Oh, for the good old days, when all that mattered was that you had the correct powerplant under the hood!

Now restoration means having everything on the car that's supposed to be there. It means interpreting the Vehicle Identification Number (VIN) to determine if anything has been changed. It also means finding, if possible, the production broadcast sheet, which details the options the car carried when it was built.

The correct engine that came with the car is a must. Putting a 428 Cobra Jet engine in a Mach 1 Mustang that was built with a 351 Cleveland makes for a hotter car, true, but the car is not "correct." Furthermore, passing it off as something that it is not for financial gain is not honest. Such fraud is a crime, but it's something that happens more and more in today's muscle car market. Have an expert check out a prospective purchase before you plunk down the money.

"All numbers match." You've seen that statement many times in muscle car advertisements. So what's it mean? Well, there are certain numbers that should be identical on the car's VIN, other numbers on the cowl tag, and still other numbers on locations of the car's power train. The muscle car clubs and registries listed in Appendices A and B will be able to provide you with invaluable information on your particular model.

After ensuring that what you're buying is the real item, it's necessary to examine the machine to roughly determine how much money is needed to restore it to the condition you desire—Concours-perfect or a daily or weekend driver. Even if it's a super-rare car, if many thousands of dollars are needed to restore it, it might not be a worthwhile purchase. Again, engaging an expert to examine the potential purchase is highly recommended.

Rust is the big villian in these 20- and 30-year-old machines, and it can damage or destroy the frame and sheet metal. Fortunately, many parts being reproduced today can make the job easier. And, of course, the junkyard might just yield that needed part, but it's getting harder and harder to find parts as the cars get older. Check out the list of manufacturers in Appendix C for help.

WAR STORIES FROM THE MUSCLE FRONT

Sometimes the price for a muscle car seems too good to be true—that is, until you see it. Dan Holtz of Ohio once heard about a highly desirable 1970 440 Six-Pack 'Cuda. To give you an idea of what he got, he paid the owner only $50.

"It was a total disaster and had been thoroughly thrashed at a dragstrip for years," recalls Holtz. "It had then sat in a barn for six years. Mice had eaten the interior and made a nest in the heater box." It took him seven years to restore the car.

Ron Hendricks faced an equal challenge with his '66 Mercury 390 Comet. It too was found in a barn, and squirrels (along with the ever-present mice) had made it their home.

"It was missing the floor panels," says Hendricks, "the bumpers were smashed, and the rear quarters were completely gone." But since Hendricks was able to determine that most of the car was still there, that, along with the fact that only 15,970 were produced, made the purchase worthwhile.

Chris Coulson of Winnipeg, Manitoba, says that his 1970 440 'Cuda is but one of 12 Six-Barrel convertibles produced that year. The motivation for the restoration was there.

"I bought the car for twenty-four hundred Canadian dollars in 1982 and it was really beat. The wife was not happy at all with me for buying the car. She just couldn't believe I paid that kind of money for it." I'm happy to announce that after Coulson's outstanding restoration, his wife is now one of the car's biggest fans.

Larry Gordon faced an even tougher challenge with his now-gorgeous '70 Challenger R/T. "It cost me four hundred dollars, which certainly was no

The Camaro Nationals in Dayton, Ohio.

bargain when I got it. The body had for some reason been beaten on with a large hammer and the top had been stomped flat. The owner was ready to haul it to the junkyard when I made the offer and he took it. I think he must have wondered if I was crazy." Once again, the fact that it was a loaded big-block car made Larry think it would be worth the effort.

Jim Mitchell sheepishly admits that the guy he bought his 340 Duster from really didn't know the value of the car. "But then again, neither did I. It was the pink color of the car that I really bought the car for." He learned later that there were only about 20 of the cars built in Panther Pink.

Gary Board of Columbus, Ohio, says he figures that the former owner of his 1970 Super Cobra Jet Torino probably thought he was taking this young kid. "I knew how rare the car was even though I was only 16 at the time. It was terrible to look at and took me five years to restore the car. I knew that I could do the job."

There are still muscle car bargains out there to be found. Maybe there's one in that barn just down the road. You can also see many of these cars still driving down the street every day. Others can be found out at the local drag strip.

In case you haven't gotten the message yet, here's that final word of warning again: Let the buyer beware!

Muscle Car Clubs

GENERAL MOTORS
Buick

GS CLUB OF AMERICA
1213 Gornto Road
Valdosta, GA 31602

BUICK CLUB OF AMERICA
PO Box 898
Garden Grove, CA 92642

Chevrolet

CAMARO OWNERS OF AMERICA, INC.
701 N. Keyser Avenue
Scranton, PA 18508

COPO CAMARO ORGANIZATION
PO Box 1036
Lombard, IL 60148

UNITED STATES CAMARO CLUB
3944 Indian Ripple Road
Dayton, OH 45440

NATIONAL CHEVELLE OWNERS ASSOCIATION
PO Box 5014
Greensboro, SC 27435

CHEVELLE OWNERS CLUB
PO Box 721
Rialto, CA 92376

NATIONAL NOSTALGIC NOVA
PO Box 2344
York, PA 17405

NATIONAL 409 CHEVY CLUB
2510 East 14th Street
Long Beach, CA 90804

NATIONAL IMPALA ASSOCIATION
PO Box 5014
Greensboro, NC 27435

LATE GREAT CHEVYS '58–'64
PO Box 17824
Orlando, FL 32860

NATIONAL MONTE CARLO CLUB
PO Box 187
Independence, KY 41051

CORVETTE CLUB OF AMERICA
PO Box 30379
Washington, DC 20814

NATIONAL CORVETTE OWNERS ASSOCIATION
PO Box 777A
Falls Church, VA 22046

NATIONAL COUNCIL OF CORVETTE CLUBS, INC.
PO Box 5032
Lafayette, IN 47903

Oldsmobile

OLDSMOBILE PERFORMANCE CHAPTER
PO Box 4563
Chicago, IL 60680

OLDSMOBILE CLUB OF AMERICA
PO Box 16216
Lansing, MI 48901

HURST OLDS CLUB OF AMERICA
3623 Burchfield Drive
Lansing, MI 48901

NATIONAL 4-4-2 OWNERS CLUB
PO Box 594
Kirkland, WA 98033

Pontiac

GTO ASSOCIATION OF AMERICA
1634 Briarson Drive
Saganaw, MI 60152

THE JUDGE GTO INTERNATIONAL CLUB
114 Prince George Drive
Hampton, VA 23669

TRANS AM CLUB OF AMERICA
PO Box 33085
North Royalton, OH 44133

NATIONAL FIREBIRD CLUB
PO Box 11238
Chicago, IL 60611

NATIONAL 4-4-2 OWNERS CLUB
PO Box 594
Kirkland, WA 98033

FORD

FAIRLANE CLUB OF AMERICA
721 Drexel Ave.
Drexel Hill, PA 19026

PERFORMANCE FORD CLUB OF AMERICA
PO Box 32
Ashville, OH 43103

MUSTANG OWNERS INTERNATIONAL
2720 Tennessee Northeast
Albuquerque, NM 87110

FALCON CLUB OF AMERICA
629 N. Hospital Drive
Jacksonville, AR 72076

SHELBY AMERICAN AUTOMOBILE CLUB
22 Olmstead Road
West Redding, CT 06896

MUSTANG CLUB OF AMERICA
PO Box 447
Lithonia, GA 30058

COUGAR CLUB OF AMERICA
0-4211 N. 120th Avenue
Holland, MI 49424

THE RANCHERO CLUB
1339 Beverly Road
Port Vue, PA 15133

AMERICAN COMET CLUB-UNITED SPOILERS OF AMERICA
Route 4, Box 116
Alexandria, IN

THE CLASSIC COMET CLUB OF AMERICA
419 North Fulton Street
Allentown, PA 18102

CHRYSLER

RAPID TRANSIT SYSTEM
1513 South 121st
Omaha, NE 68144

D.A.R.T.S.
PO Box 9
Wethersfield, CT 06109

BARRACUDA/'CUDA OWNERS CLUB
RD 4, Box 61
Northhampton, PA 18067

ROAD RUNNER & GTX ASSOCIATION
PO Box 55
Midland, VA 22728

NATIONAL HEMI OWNERS ASSOCIATION
3836 N 101st Street
Wauwatosa, WI 53222

MOPAR MUSCLE CLUB INTERNATIONAL
Route 9, Box 18
Lockport, IL 60441

CHRYSLER 300 CLUB INTERNATIONAL
19 Donegal Court
Ann Arbor, MI 48104

WINGED WARRIORS
6851 San Diego Drive
Budena Park, CA 90620

DAYTONA/SUPERBIRD AUTO CLUB
13717 West Green Meadow drive
New Berlin, WI 53151

MOPAR SCAT PACK CLUB
PO Box 2303
Dearborn, MI 48123

AMERICAN MOTORS

NATIONAL AMERICAN MOTORS DRIVERS AND RACERS ASSOCIATION
923 Plainfield Road
Countryside, IL 60525

AMERICAN MOTORS OWNERS ASSOCIATION
517 New Hampshire
Portage, MI 49081

AMX/JAVELIN CLUB OF AMERICA
PO Box 9307
Daytona Beach, FL 32020

GENERAL

NATIONAL MUSCLE CAR ASSOCIATION
3402 Democrat Road
Memphis, TN 38118

Muscle Car Registries

GENERAL MOTORS

BUICK GSX REGISTRY
3843 Regent Drive
Dallas, TX 75229

ZL1 CAMARO REGISTRY
PO Box 1036
Lombard, IL 60148

CAMARO PACE REGISTRY
3944 Indian Ripple Road
Dayton, OH 45440

Z-16 CHEVELLE REGISTRY
1907 Blvd
Colonial Heights, VA 23834

OLDS RALLYE 350 REGISTRY
37 Georgia Street
Crawford, NJ 07016

OLDS 4-4-2 REGISTRY
1000 South 19th Street
Arlington, VA 22202

FORD

428 MUSTANG REGISTRY
6890 Plainfield
Dearborn Heights, MI 48127

1965-1970 SHELBY REGISTRY
22 Oldstead Road
West Redding, CT 06896

1969–1970 MACH I REGISTRY
10824 13th Street
Edmonton, Alberta, Canada T5M 1L9

BOSS 302 REGISTRY
1817 Janet Avenue
Lebanon, PA 17042-1845

BOSS 351 REGISTRY
PO Box 26644
Jacksonville, FL 32218

BOSS 429 REGISTRY
4228 Conklin
Spokane, WA 99203

CALIFORNIA SPECIAL/HIGH COUNTRY SPECIAL REGISTRY
PO Box 2013
El Macero, CA 95618

MUSTANG GT REGISTRY
16830 Stahelin
Detroit, MI 48219

TWISTER SPECIAL REGISTRY
7520 N.W. Rochester
Topeka, KS 66617

'71 429 MUSTANG REGISTRY
6250 Germantown Pike
Dayton, OH 45418

COUGAR/ELIMINATOR/XR-7/GTE REGISTRY
919 Willowbrook, Dept MCR
Allen, TX 75002

7-LITER (GALAXIE) REGISTRY
17 Verdum Drive
Akron, OH 44312

SPOILER-TALLADEGA REGISTRY
629 West Sylvania Ave.
Toledo, OH 43612

CHRYSLER

AAR 'CUDA REGISTRY
861 Kent Street
Portland, MI 48875

DODGE CHARGER REGISTRY
109 Carver Place
Grafton, VA 23692

DODGE CHALLENGER REGISTRY (1970–1974 R/Ts, R/T SEs)
PO Box 132
Barrington, NJ 08007-1651

AMC

SC/RAMBLER REGISTRY
1646 Clairmont Way
Atlanta, GA 30329

Muscle Car Restoration Suppliers

GENERAL MOTORS

CAMARO COUNTRY
18591 Centennial Road
Marshall, MI 49068
(Camaro parts)

CAROLINA CAMARO
Route 3, Box 24
Elon College, NC 27244
(Camaro parts)

CAMARO CONNECTION
34B Cleveland Avenue
Bay Shore, NY 11706
(Camaro parts)

KENNE-BELL OLDS
10743 Bell Court, Dpt D
Rancho Cucamongo, CA 91730
(Buick, Olds motors)

AMERICAN CUSTOM INDUSTRIES
5035 Alexis Road
Sylvania, OH 43560
(Corvette body parts)

VETTE BRAKES AND PRODUCTS
7490-30th Avenue North, Dept US
St Petersburg, FL 33710
(Corvette parts)

CLASSIC CAMARO PARTS AND ACC. INC.
16651 Gemini Lane
Huntington Beach, CA 92647
(Camaro parts)

NATIONAL PARTS DEPOT
3101 Southwest 40th Blvd
Gainesville, FL 32608
(Camaro parts)

YEAR ONE
PO Box 450131 Group USCO
Atlanta, GA 3034
(Camaro parts)

C.A.R.S. INC
1964 West 11 Mile Road
Dept RO-5
Berkley, MI 48072
(All Chevy parts)

ECKLER'S
PO Box 5637
Titusville, FL 32783
(Corvette parts)

GENUINE CLASSIC BRAKES
341 Knickerbocker Ave
Bohemia, NY 11716
(Corvette brakes)

CORVETTE PERF PRODUCTS
PO Box 6421
Evansville, IN 47719
(Corvette accessories)

CHEVELLE CLASSICS
16602 Burke Lane
Huntington Beach, CA 92647
(Chevelle parts)

JUST SUSPENSION
PO Box 167
Towaco, NJ 07082
(Corvette suspension)

CHICAGO CORVETTE SUPPLY
7322 South Archer Road
Justice, IL 60458
(Corvette parts)

TRACY PERFORMANCE
29069 Calahan
Roseville, MI 48066
(Corvette parts)

SNAKE-OYL PRODUCTS
15775 N Hillcrest
Dallas, TX 75248
(Seat belt restoration)

ZIP PRODUCTS
1250 Commercial Center
Mechanicsville, VA 23111
(Corvette radiators)

CORVETTE WAREHOUSE
204 Industry Parkway
Nicholasville, KY 40356
(Corvette interiors)

THE PADDOCK, INC
221 West Main, Box 30, Dept UC
Knightstown, IN 46148
(Camaro parts)

THE RIGHT STUFF
1369 Community Park Drive
Columbus, OH 43229
(Camaro fluid lines)

DNR Classic Automotive
2101 75th Avenue
Elmwood Park, IL 60635
(GM parts)

Z & Z Auto
233 North Lemon
Orange, CA 92666
(Camaro and Firebird parts)

Ausley's
300 South Main Street
Graham, NC 27253
(Chevelle parts)

Mid-Atlantic Performance
Box 333-MR
Simpsonville, MD 21150
(Buick and Olds parts)

Classic Car Interiors
140 Route 202
Chads Ford, PA 19317
(Buick GS interiors)

Phoenix Graphix
6925 Fifth Avenue, Ste. E-217
Scottsdale, AR 85251
(Trans Am decals)

Classic Rubber Products
6925 5th Avenue
Lake City, MI 49651
(Camaro, Firebird weatherstrips)

Specialty Olds
1727 West Cypress Street, Dept CR
Tampa, FL 33606
(Olds parts)

Auto Acc. of America
Box 427, Route 322
Boalsburg, PA 16827
(Corvette interior pkgs.)

GTOs
279 Stahl Road
Harleysville, PA 19438
(Pontiac parts)

CLASSIC REPRODUCTIONS
5315 Meeker Road
Greenville, OH 45331
(Pontiac manifolds)

TED WILLIAMS CHEVELLE
5615 State RT 45
Lisbon, OH 44432
(Chevelle/El Camino parts)

HYDRO-E-LECTRIC
48 Appleton Road
Auburn, MA 01501
(Convertible lift parts)

MPPOWER
265 Courtland Street
Lindenhurst, NY 11757
(Brakes)

USA-1
PO Box 691
Williamstown, NJ 08094
(Chevy interiors)

CUSTOM F/X FIBERGLASS
8811 Carpenter Freeway
Dallas, TX 75247
(Camaro hoods)

CUSTOM MOLD DYNAMICS
5161-R Wolfpen Pl Hill Rd
Milford, OH 45150
(Chevy/Pontiac emblems)

CHEVELLE WORLD INC.
PO Box 38H
Washington, OK 73093
(Chevelle parts)

J & M Auto Parts
RFD 5, Box 170, Dept M
Pellam, NH 03076
(Chevy parts and accessories)

Super Cars Unlimited
8029-A Southwest 17th
Portland, OR 97219
(Olds parts)

Camaro Specialties
898 East Philmore, Dept MC
East Aurora, NY 14052
(Camaro parts)

Bethel's Goat Farm
85 North 27th Street, Dept 04
San Jose, CA 95116
(GTO parts)

Chicago Camaro and Firebird
900 South 5th Avenue
Maywood, IL 60153
(Camaro and Firebird parts)

Don's East Coast Restoration
567 Hickory Street, Dept MCR
Lindenhurst, NY 11757
(Chevy parts)

Chevyland
3667 Recycle Road #8
Rancho Cordova, CA 95742
(Chevy parts)

Danchuk Manufacturing, Inc.
3221 South Halladay, Dept MR/C
Santa Ana, CA 92705
(Chevelle and El Camino parts)

Brothers Automotive
Route 3, Box 372
St Joseph, MO 64505
(Olds parts)

JIMK OSBORN REPRODUCTIONS, INC.
101A Ridgecrest Drive
Lawrenceville, GA 30245
(Restoration decals)

CURRIE ENTERPRISES
1480 "B" N Tustin Ave
Anaheim, CA 92807
(Musclecar rear ends)

SHERMAN AND ASSOC. INC.
27940 Groesbek
Roseville, MI 48066
(Body panels)

AUTO CUSTOM CARPETS, INC.
316 J Street
Anniston, AK 36202
(Carpets)

METRO MOLDED PARTS, INC.
11610 Jay Street
Minneapolis, MN 55433
(Molded rubber parts)

SUPER SPORT PARTS, INC.
7138 Maddox Road
Lathonia, GA 30058
(Chevy parts)

OBSOLETE PARTS COMPANY
524 Hazel Avenue
Nashville, GA 31639
(Chevy parts)

SPECIALTY OLDS
1727 West Cypress St
Tampa, FL 33606
(Olds parts)

STEVE'S CAMAROS
1197 San Mateo Avenue
San Bruno, CA 94066
(Camaro/Firebird parts)

CARS
Pearl Street
Neshanic, NJ 08853
(Buick parts)

FORTIER'S CORVETTES, INC
8040 South Jennings Road
Swartz Creek, MI 48473
(Corvette parts)

FORD

KEN'S FORD PARTS
949 North Cataract Ave.
San Dimas, CA 91773
(Ford parts)

BRANDA MUSTANG PARTS
1434 East Pleasant Valley Blvd.
Altoona, PA 16602
(Mustang/Shelby parts)

HARRIS MUSTANG SUPPLY
1922 Bancroft Street
Charlotte, NC 28206
(Mustang/Shelby parts)

SEMO MUSTANG
Highway 25-Route Z
Gordonville, MO 63752
(Ford/Mustang parts)

WILD WEST MUSTANG RANCH
22909 Woodinville Sno. Hwy
Woodinville, WA 98072
(Mustang/Cougar)

AUTO KRAFTERS
PO Box 618/Route 617W
Timberville, VA 22853
(Torino stripe kits)

STANG-IT
1134B Meadow Lane
Concord, CA 94520
(Mustang/Cougar parts)

COBRA RESTORERS LIMITED
3099 Carter Circle
Kennasaw, GA 30144
(Cobra engines/parts)

SACRAMENTO MUSTANG
5710 Auburn Blvd., No 23
Sacramento, CA 95841
(Mustang parts)

LARRY'S T-BIRD & MUSTANG PARTS
511 South Raymond Avenue
Fullerton, CA 92631
(Mustang parts)

RACER WALSH COMPANY
5906 Macy Avenue, Dept 14
Jacksonville, FL 32211
(Ford parts)

DENNIS CARPENTER FORD REPROD.
PO Box 26398
Charlotte, NC 28221-6398
(Ford weatherstriping)

B&A FORD PERFORMANCE INC.
PO Box 6553
Fort Smith, Arkansas 72906
(Boss intake manifolds)

THE PADDOCK, INC
221 West Main, Dept 30
Knightstown, IN 46148
(Mustang parts)

MUSTANGS UNLIMITED, INC.
185 Adams Street
Manchester, CN 06040
(Cougar/Mustang parts)

STAINLESS STEEL BRAKES CORP.
11470 Main Road
Clarence, NY 14031
(Ford brakes)

CALIFORNIA PONY CARS
8460 Red Oak Street
Rancho Cucamonga, CA 91730
(Ford steering wheels)

MUSTANG CLASSICS
2030 Vineyard Avenue, Suite A
Escondido, CA 92025
(Mustang parts)

JUST SUSPENSION
PO Box 167
Towaco, NJ 07082
(Ford suspension kits)

GT PERFORMANCE FORD
2498 Yatesville Road
Penn Yan, NJ 14527
(Ford parts)

FORD PARTS STORE
4925 Ford Road, Box 226
Bryan, OH 43506
(Ford parts)

WALKER AND BATTAT FORD
500 Hebron Road
Newark, OH 43055
(351 oil pans/parts)

STREET AND PERFORMANCE
Route 5, No 1 Hot Rod Lane
Mena, AR 71953
(Ford parts)

POWER SOURCE
Country Plaza, Hwy 29
Greer, SC 29651
(Ford perf. parts)

MCCARVILLE FORD
2686 Middle Country Road
Centereach, NY 11720
(Ford parts)

FORD MAN'S MUSTANGS AND AUTO.
10401 Royal Pine
Houston, TX 77093
(Ford parts)

CHRYSLER

CHICAGO CONNECTION
6707 West Archer Ave
Chicago, IL 60638
(MOPAR parts)

MOPAR PERFORMANCE
3021 4th Street NW
Albuquerque, NM 87107
(MOPAR parts)

MOTOR CITY ORIGINALS, INC
16094 Common Road
Roseville, MI 48066
(MOPAR parts)

STENCILS & STRIPES UNLIMITED
1108 S Cresent Avenue
Park Ridge, IL 60068
(Tape and stripe kits)

R/T SPECIALTIES
691 West Ray Road #4
Chandler, AR 85224
(Trim pieces)

MOPAR PERFORMANCE
PO Box 388
South San Francisco, CA 94083
('60 – '70 E-body parts)

HARDEN'S MUSCLE CAR WORLD
PO Box 306
Lexington, MO 64067
(MOPAR trim)

KOLLER DODGE
1565 West Ogden Avenue
Naperville, IL 60540
(MOPAR parts)

JUST SUSPENSION
PO Box 167
Towaco, NJ 07082
(Suspension kits)

YEAR ONE INC.
PO Box 129
Tucker, GA 30085
(MOPAR parts)

AUTO BODY SPECIALTIES, INC.
PO Box 455, Route 66
Middlefield, CT 06455
(Exterior trim)

AUTOMOTIVE PERFORMANCE SPL.
755 North 10th Street
San Jose, CA 95112
(Powertrain parts)

CHALLENGER CLASSICS INC.
39500 14 Mile Road
Walled Lake, MI 48088
(Challenger parts)

NSI PERFORMANCE CENTER
PO Box 4021
Decatur, IN 46733
(MOPAR parts)

CORK'S AUTOMOTIVE REPAIR
105 Savonne
Scott, LA 70583
(New/Used MOPAR parts)

HAMBURGER'S PERF. PARTS
5 Powder Horn Drive
Warren, NJ 07060
(Motor parts)

AUTO CUSTOM CARPETS INC.
PO Box 1167
Anniston, AL 36202
(MOPAR interiors)

SHERMAN & ASSOCIATES
28460 Groesbeck Hwy
Roseville, MI 48066
(Body panels)

MP POWER MASTER
265 Cortland Street
Lindenhurst, NY 11757
(Brake parts)

EDWARDS BROS. INC
14223 Hawthorne Ct.
Fountain Hills, AR 85268
(Front suspension kits)

Index

Other Bestsellers of Related Interest

TROUBLESHOOTING AND REPAIRING POWER TOOLS—Homer L. Davidson

Improve the performance and lengthen the lifespan of your power tools with this comprehensive guide to the care and repair of electric and battery-powered tools. Using clear instructions and work-in-progress photographs, it shows you how to extend the life of everything from cordless screwdrivers to electric mowers through simple cleaning, lubricating, and sharpening procedures. Most of the procedures detailed can be accomplished using common tools, and all can be followed safely and successfully. 256 pages, 311 illustrations. Book No. 3347, $17.95 paperback, $26.95 hardcover

DECKS AND PATIOS: Designing and Building Outdoor Living Spaces—Edward A. Baldwin

This handsome book will show you step by step how to take advantage of outdoor space. It's a comprehensive guide to designing and building decks and patios that fit the style of your home and the space available. You'll find coverage of a variety of decks, patios, walkways, and stairs. Baldwin helps you design your outdoor project, and then shows you how to accomplish every step from site preparation through finishing and preserving your work to ensure many years of enjoyment. 152 pages, 180 illustrations. Book No. 3326, $16.95 paperback, $26.95 hardcover

TROUBLESHOOTING AND REPAIRING VCRS—2nd Edition—Gordon McComb

This book has helped more than 80,000 VCR owners keep their machines working at peak performance. With this book and a basic set of tools, you can handle most VCR problems quickly and easily—from simple parts cleaning and lubrication to repairing power supply and circuitry malfunctions. This revised second edition updates the bestselling original volume with the most recent technological advances. 432 pages, 186 illustrations. Book No. 3777, $19.95 paperback, $32.95 hardcover

HOW TO GET MORE MILES PER GALLON IN THE 1990s—Robert Sikorsky

This new edition of a best-seller features a wealth of commonsense tips and techniques for improving gas mileage by as much as 100 percent. Sikorsky details specific gas-saving strategies that will greatly reduce aerodynamic drag and increase engine efficiency. New to this edition is coverage of the latest fuel-conserving automotive equipment, fuel additives, engine treatments, lubricants, and maintenance procedures that can help save energy. 184 pages, 39 illustrations. Book No. 3793, $7.95 paperback, $16.95 hardcover

RIP-OFF TIP-OFFS: Winning the Auto Repair Game—Robert Sikorsky

Don't get ripped off when you take your car for repairs. This book gives you the ammunition to stop repair scams before they start. Sikorsky exposes popular tactics used by cheats and describes how to ensure a fair deal. If you have been ripped off, he tells you how to complain effectively—both to get your money back and to put the charlatans out of business for good. But most importantly, Sikorsky tells how to avoid getting burned in the first place by learning how your car works and by keeping it in good condition. 140 pages, 29 illustrations. Book No. 3572, $9.95 paperback, $16.95 hardcover

THE WEEKEND MECHANIC'S AUTO BODY REPAIR GUIDE—Robert Grossblatt and Billy Boynton

Dings, dents, bumps, crunches, and crashes have happened to cars since the discovery that they were *not* indestructible. To avoid the typical repair-bill shock to your system, follow this professional advice and do your own body repairs and painting. This is the manual you need to take you from "oh, no!" to the final buff on your undetectable repair. 160 pages, 140 illustrations. Book No. 3497, $13.95 paperback, $23.95 hardcover

TV REPAIR FOR BEGINNERS—4th Edition
—George Zwick and Homer L. Davidson

This updated version contains information about new technologies not covered in the first three editions, including the many TV circuits that have appeared in the last 10 years. You'll look at X-ray protection circuits, scan-derived voltages, saw filter networks, high-voltage shutdowns, chopper power supplies, sand-castle generators, switched-mode power supplies, stereo sound, on-screen display, and surface-mounted components. 360 pages, 303 illustrations. Book No. 3627, $19.95 paperback, $29.95 hardcover

YOUR DREAM VACATION HOME
—Mary S. Ludwig

Buy a vacation home, use it as a rental property, and write off a large portion of the expense—while still enjoying vacations there! With this handy guide, you'll know how to take full advantage of these tax breaks. The book thoroughly explains how to buy and use a vacation home for recreation and profit. You'll learn how to select, finance, rent, exchange, and sell vacation property. 240 pages, illustrated. Book No. 3687, $14.95 paperback only

Prices Subject to Change Without Notice.

Look for These and Other TAB Books at Your Local Bookstore

To Order Call Toll Free 1-800-822-8158
(in PA, AK, and Canada call 717-794-2191)

or write to TAB Books, Blue Ridge Summit, PA 17294-0840.

Title	Product No.	Quantity	Price

☐ Check or money order made payable to TAB Books

Charge my ☐ VISA ☐ MasterCard ☐ American Express

Acct. No. _____ Exp. _____

Signature: _____

Name: _____

Address: _____

City: _____

State: _____ Zip: _____

Subtotal $ _____

Postage and Handling
($3.00 in U.S., $5.00 outside U.S.) $ _____

Add applicable state and local
sales tax $ _____

TOTAL $ _____

TAB Books catalog free with purchase; otherwise send $1.00 in check or money order and receive $1.00 credit on your next purchase.

Orders outside U.S. must pay with international money order in U.S. dollars.

TAB Guarantee: If for any reason you are not satisfied with the book(s) you order, simply return it (them) within 15 days and receive a full refund.
BC